Always Protect Your Behind
A Life Guide for Young Adults
Or Misguided Old Ones

by

Barbara L. Ayers

TP

TELEMACHUS PRESS

This book is for your reading enjoyment only. The suggestions offered should only be implemented after careful review by a trained professional as part of a program specifically designed for you and your situation.

Published by Telemachus Press, LLC
http://www.telemachuspress.com

Library of Congress Control Number: 2014943367

ISBN: 978-1-941536-34-6 (eBook)
ISBN: 978-1-941536-35-3 (Paperback)

Version 2015.01.01

Printed in the United States of America

10 9 8 7 6 5 4 3 2 1

Dedicated to the beautiful young women in my life
Kimberly and Lindsay

Take time to work … it is the price of success
Take time to think … it is the source of power
Take time to play … it is the secret of youth
Take time to read … it is the fountain of wisdom
Take time to be friendly … it is the road to happiness
Take time to dream … it is hitching your wagon to a star
Take time to love and be loved … it is the privilege of the gods
Take time to look around … it is too short a day to be selfish
Take time to laugh … it is the music of the soul.
Old Irish Prayer

Table of Contents

Congratulations!

YOU FINALLY HAVE the opportunity to leave home, to venture out into the world! Or maybe you've been out there a while, even years, and seem to find yourself in need of some advice—a gentle kick in the behind because you forgot to protect it.

You are not alone. Most of us have had to experience the often difficult learning curve along the road towards adulthood. The things in life that we encounter daily can be frightening, intimidating, and discouraging. Even some of the seemingly simple activities can find a way to create havoc in our normal routines. But, they can also be exciting, exhilarating, and life changing.

Even with the multitude of lessons that life throws your way, it's important that you get up and venture out there into the world with the full force of who you are and what you want out of life. Nobody else is able to do this for you. It's about getting to know what you want and what you can do for yourself and the world with as few pitfalls as possible.

Some days you feel like the cat and
some days you feel like the mouse ...

You now have in your hands a book that has been developed after countless, enlightening discussions with so many amazing people who have found difficulties along their own journeys towards becoming adults and trying to make it towards their desired life goals. This book is presented not just as snippets of advice, but as a tool to help you avoid the same exact problems so many of us have experienced. Most of these same issues have been repeated often and reflected upon throughout history. It only makes sense to learn from those who have come before us ...

By no means does this book contain an exhaustive list of common mistakes. Nor is this book meant to point fingers at parents, teachers, or caregivers for their failure to confer to any of us all of the warnings needed before venturing out into the big, wide world. Society of today has far too many rules, fine print, and technology for any one person to have experienced everything or even imparted most of it to other people. And so, it would be wise of you to be able to take the experiences of others and learn from them without the stress and pains from the actual experiences.

By these methods we may learn wisdom:
first, by reflection which is noblest;
second by imitation, which is the easiest;
and third, by experience, which is the bitterest.
Confucius, 551–479 BCE
Chinese Social and Political Philosopher and Educator

Knowledge empowers. The hope is that you will be able to use this information proffered to evade some of the more specific errors and to create a more satisfying life for yourself and hence a better world in which to live. Who wouldn't want this?

There are many things that you can learn on your own if you pay attention. You have many decisions to make. Some big, others small. But, even the ones that seem small can have a huge, enormous impact if you do not pay attention and use any knowledge wisely, with an open mind.

If you expect a book with "no duh's" or "what the heck were you thinking?" Stop now. You will not be barraged with personal insults or profanity; which, by the way, could easily have been inserted anywhere within these pages. This is not the point of the book. It's a straight forward guide, with useful information and points that don't need to be presented with such drivel or lack of truly meaningless adjectives or adverbs. They would add only disrespect to the reader, the writer, and those amazing people who provided much insight into what it takes to become an adult who can function successfully in the world.

It is an obvious statement that every person will feel and approach any major life change differently, especially growing up and being out on your own. Some individuals may think of the transition as a chance to get away from those horrid parental rules seemingly invented to impose unwanted restrictions on life. Others may consider it as an opportunity to spread their wings; an adventure into the unknown to test their ability to be successful in the world. Still, we all know that there will be those who have been "out there" and desperately want to crawl back under the covers, hoping to delay or reverse the inevitable. Well, it's finally time to crawl out and create a life worth living …

Got direction?

Your attitude, common sense, and observational skills are the three key elements that will determine what happens during your own personal journey.

Keep a positive and inquisitive attitude and you will attract good people and good things. It's about making a presence and having the confidence to do so appropriately. You will become a much more interesting person with whom people encounter and want to be around. Negativity and narrow mindedness lead to loneliness and a life riddled with problems.

The control center of your life is your attitude.
Author Unknown

Most of us have heard the term street smarts. The term has been grossly misused by comparing it to book smarts. That alone lends a limited and dangerous aspect to the meaning. The complete underlying definition of the term holds that it's our offensive and defensive thinking <u>as well as</u> awareness that lead to successful self-protection responses within specific situations. It's the practical application of something we know as common sense. Wisdom comes from good use of common sense. It is not just instincts, but also the knowledge accumulated from so many sources, including formal education. We are always learning. It's when you refuse to learn that you can find yourself stuck in a rut.

Common-sense in an uncommon degree is what the world calls wisdom.
Samuel Taylor Coleridge, 1772–1834
British Poet, Critic, Philosopher and Founder of the English Romantic Movement

This common sense is fine-tuned by your adaptability of behavior to ever changing circumstances. It's not just location specific, but rather situation specific, requiring the fluidity of responses to any given situation. It's your reactions within any given situation that can determine any outcome. Moving forward or flailing.

At the same time, a limited exposure to a wide variety of environments will result in fewer experiences to test and to incorporate any new responses into your repertoire. A person can become stuck in patterns of behavior that become inept or inappropriate responses when put into new situations in either old or new environments. Being open to new experiences means you will be open to learning.

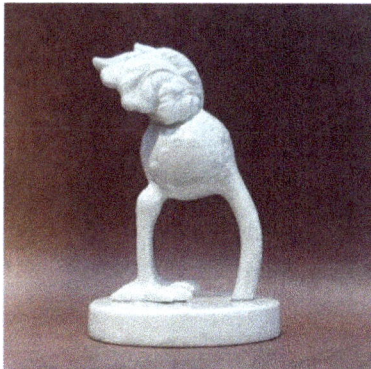

Pull your head out of the sand ...

Everyone must develop a certain level of observational proficiency that is required to be able to learn the necessary skills to adapt to new environments or ever changing circumstances. Learning never stops. It is a continual process, measured by a person's level of awareness and use of common sense.

A man should look for what is,
and not for what he thinks should be.
Albert Einstein, 1879–1955
German Theoretical Physicist

In life you won't want to miss a thing. You won't. But, it's not enough to simply see, you have to be aware. You need to be open-minded as you go out into the world—with your eyes wide open. This will help to positively enhance your attitude, common sense, and observational skills. Opportunities are lost by those who live with blinders on or a rigid mindset. It doesn't hurt to take a hard look at yourself from time to time or those with whom you surround yourself.

During a visit to the mental asylum, a visitor asked the Director what the criterion
was which defined whether or not a patient should be institutionalized.
"Well," said the Director, "we fill up a bathtub, then we offer a teaspoon, a teacup,
and a bucket to the patient and ask him or her to empty the bathtub."
"Oh, I understand," said the visitor. "A normal person would use the
bucket because it's bigger than the spoon or the teacup."
"No," said the Director, "A normal person would pull the plug.
Do you want a bed near the window?"
Author Unknown

What is the key to a successful and happy life? To use sound practical judgment in what you say and do. This develops directly from a person's well-developed attitude, common sense and observational skills. It is defined as an individual's character.

Success is getting what you want;
happiness is wanting what you get.
Dale Carnegie, 1888–1955
American Writer and Lecturer

Motives direct one's judgments and say a lot about the 'what and whys' of a person's behavior. Try talking less and listening more. Sit on your ego. In other words sometimes it's best to keep your mouth shut, observe, and absorb. More often than not it will keep you out of trouble and you may gain something from what's going on around you.

A cynic is a man who knows the price of everything and the value of nothing.
Oscar Wilde, 1854–1900
Irish Writer and Poet

Everything begins with baby steps. Hopefully this book will assist you in finding a few to guide you in making some good future decisions for yourself. Try to keep focused yet flexible. It's all about creating a good life for yourself and, in the process, the human race of which you are a part.

One of the most beautiful gifts in the world is the gift of encouragement.
When someone encourages you, that person helps you over a threshold
you might otherwise never have crossed on your own.
John O'Donohue, 1956–2008
Irish Poet and Philosopher

The Real World of Work and School

WORK AND SCHOOL are both an educational experience. And, in a basic sense, you get paid for both. Your decision to go on to a higher education or to enter the workforce is influenced by many factors. For some, it's the expense. Others didn't make the grade. Still, others want to experience the world before buckling down to more studious activities.

> *The most important function of education at any level*
> *is to develop the personality of the individual*
> *and the significance of his life to himself and to others.*
> *Grayson Kirk, 1903–1997*
> *President of Columbia University, State Department Advisor, and*
> *Instrumental in forming the United Nations*

It doesn't matter which road you choose, you will always be exposed to new learning experiences. These will present you with so many opportunities to evolve in thought and behavior and to become more successful in identifying and achieving your personal goals.

> *The only person who is educated*
> *is the one who has learned*
> *how to learn and change.*
> *Carl Rogers, 1902–1987*
> *American Psychologist*

Be proud of your dreams and accomplishments …

There are many avenues open to you in making a decision on attending school, going to work, or doing both. Always look for the options that both your life and society around you offers. It's not about following the crowd or your friends, but doing what you need to do. It's your future. Let your friends be responsible for their own. Your success cannot be determined by their dreams and aspirations. You have your own.

Do not go where the path may lead;
go instead where there is no path and leave a trail.
Ralph Waldo Emerson, 1803–1882
American Poet, Lecturer and Essayist

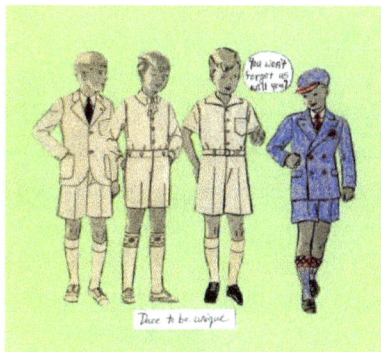

A perusal of the internet or even a magazine that you frequently read or attending a college or work fair may spark an idea or two. If you attend school, what will you study? If you get a job, what field will you go into? So many people today switch interests and careers midstride, so don't think you will be trapped once you decide. Use your imagination. Be open-minded to the unexpected opportunities that come your way.

> *You have brains in your head.*
> *You have feet in your shoes.*
> *You can steer yourself in any direction you choose.*
> *You're on your own.*
> *And you know what you know.*
> *You are the guy who'll decide where to go.*
> *Dr. Seuss, 1904–1991*
> *American Writer and Cartoonist*

If it's the money preventing you from going right into college, it's important that you understand what financial assistance may be available to you. Take the initiative and be actively involved in finding this information. Persevere in locating the right financial plan for you. Your search could be a valuable stepping stone to discovering what may interest you as a career choice. You may surprise yourself and find something you had never previously thought of or ever considered possible.

> *Lack of money is no obstacle.*
> *Lack of an idea is an obstacle.*
> *Ken Hakuta, 1950–*
> *Japanese-American Inventor and Television Personality*

It's sad that there are so many scholarships up for grabs that are never applied for and remain unused year after year. Some can be unconventionally specialized and obscured from average searches. They may be specific to a state, school, or even sub-discipline of a particular field of study. Not every guidance counselor has the knowledge of where to locate them all. But it can be a good start to consult with one. Especially one located at the school you want to attend. So many people have found just such assistance invaluable. Get creative in your search for a scholarship and don't give up on finding a way to attend school if that is one of your goals.

The most important aspect of freedom of speech is freedom to learn.
All education is a continuous dialogue —
questions and answers that pursue every problem on the horizon.
That is the essence of academic freedom.
William Orville Douglas, 1898–1980
Longest Serving Associate Justice on the US Supreme Court

Know that many class schedules will allow you to both work and attend school. There are quite a few advantageous degrees that individuals can obtain by simply taking classes on the internet. Sometimes you may have to show up for a few classes or exams on campus, so be aware of these potential situations. Many employers will work with you to permit the time for your education without any drawbacks or penalties.

The field of study you choose may have a paid internship program available. Do the research. Contact people who might have information that could lead you to other people who would know of such possibilities. Educators, businesses, and individuals working in the field are often good resources.

The object of education is to prepare the young
to educate themselves throughout their lives.
Robert M. Hutchins, 1899–1977
American Educator and Writer

If you failed to make the grade to attend a college or university, there are always alternatives to the old traditional route. There are so many trade schools, apprenticeship programs, and specialized educational institutions that exist in this day and age. What about college via the military route? Think. Investigate. What could work for you?

Twenty years from now you will be more disappointed
by the things that you didn't do than by the ones you did do.
So throw off the bowlines.
Sail away from the safe harbor.
Catch the trade winds in your sails.
Explore. Dream. Discover.
Mark Twain, 1835–1910
American Humorist, Writer and Lecturer

I keep physically and mentally fit with the military.
When I get out, I will get my advanced degree
using the GI Bill and housing allowance.

It's crucial to remember that communication and timing are very important no matter what type of educational institution you choose to attend. Many young adults have experienced the mistake of not keeping on top of things.

Contact with the school will need to be initiated and maintained. The importance of following a timeline cannot be stressed enough. Recommendations from former teachers or counselors should be secured. There are deadlines to be met for things such as registration for attendance, housing, financial aid, transcript ordering, and writing essays. Make yourself a checklist of the requirements for every institution to which you plan to apply. Refer to it often.

You may need to register and take entrance exams. It is a wise choice to take an exam more than once; as you can often select the highest score to send to the educational institution you want to attend. This fact often blows over us because we are so stressed out over having to take "an exam." Many individuals do better the second time around. Whether it's that they gain a better feel for what the testing situation is like and, hence, the test anxiety is reduced. Who knows? You have nothing to lose by taking exams more than once if the opportunity is offered.

The difference between school and life?
In school, you're taught a lesson and then given a test.
In life, you're given a test that teaches you a lesson.
Tom Bodett, 1955–
American Author, Voice Actor, and Radio Host

Electing to go right into the job market instead of schooling often gives an individual the time to grow and discover what interests them. It also can allow for the saving of money for future choices, whether it be advancing one's education or starting a business. For some, this is the right decision. Only you can decide this for yourself.

To find out what one is fitted to do,
and to secure an opportunity to do it,
is the key to happiness.
John Dewey, 1859–1952
American Philosopher, Psychologist, and Educational Reformer

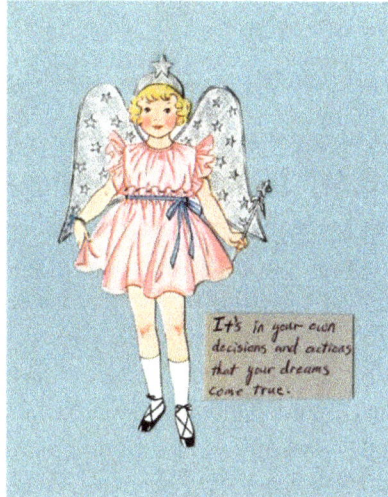

It's in your own decisions and actions that your dreams come true.

In finding the right position in the workplace, you will do much of the same investigating as the person who continues on to school. There is nothing more frustrating than working at a job you don't like. Start by making a list of what you like to do. Take a look at the want ads in the various newspapers, magazines, and on the internet. Put together a resume and cover letter of introduction. Doing so will make you look like a serious candidate to most prospective employers.

Work is love made visible.
And if you cannot work with love but only with distaste,
it is better that you should leave your work
and sit at the gate of the temple
and take alms of those who work with joy.
Khalil Gilbran, 1883–1931
Lebanese American Writer, Artist, and Poet

Preparing for Life

NO MATTER WHETHER you choose work or school, there is still a level of common sense that a person must follow to be successful and to move towards achieving goals and creating an enjoyable life. Behavior reveals a side of a person's character that will either promote or hinder that success within any particular organization or social group. It's important to take a serious interest in what you are doing at work and school, and life in general. Have the courage and ability to multi-task as well as to develop and maintain a practical level of focus, flexibility, and patience. This will usually take you to where you want to be.

Education is a social process.
Education is growth.
Education is, not a preparation for life;
education is life itself.
John Dewey, 1859–1952
American Philosopher, Psychologist, and Educational Reformer

First off, read manuals, brochures, paperwork, and such completely and thoroughly. Don't be shy about taking notes and asking questions. A good administrator, teacher, or employer will have the answers or know where to find them for you. If they don't, you have either asked the wrong questions or the wrong person. Self-motivation is usually admired and opens doors.

It is better to be prepared for an opportunity and not have one
than to have an opportunity and not be prepared.
Whitney Moore Young, 1921–1971
American Civil Rights Leader

Above all, be on time and be prepared whether for work or school. Go to bed early and get up early. A good night's sleep allows better thinking skills. This is the same with a good breakfast. Rising early allows ample time to become alert, to bathe, and to get nourishment. It enables you to meet the day with a good attitude and greater focus.

Early to bed and early to rise makes a man healthy, wealthy, and wise.
Benjamin Franklin, 1706–1790
American Author, Diplomat, Inventor, Physicist, and Politician

Allowing enough time for traveling to work or school creates less stress and anxiety. One can never know when to anticipate delays en route. Ultimately, with a relaxed start, you will be more focused on things and can have the potential for developing a more meaningful day. You might even have time at your destination to chat with people and make potential connections because you have time before the beginning of the days' commitments.

So be alert and open to any opportunity that can arise in early arrivals to work or school. Opportunities sometimes do appear and we don't even notice—or unfortunately we realize it after the event has passed. Often it's too late to act upon it … Then we feel that "oh my gosh, I should have said this or inquired about that." Perhaps you will have missed a chance for advancement in your career.

> *Chance favors only the prepared mind.*
> *Louis Pasteur, 1822–1895*
> *French Chemist and Microbiologist*

A good night's sleep is refreshing. But, sometimes we need to get out and join in the night's social scene. And even to choose to stay out late. Just make good decisions in how, where, when, and with whom you chose to do this. So many adults can tell you that the number of potentially dangerous variables increases after bar hours and on weekends. Too often, the end result of just being out or partying at a very late hour can be injury or death. You don't have to be drinking to have a drunken encounter with a person or vehicle.

> *But the greatest love—the love above all loves,*
> *Even greater than that of a mother …*
> *Is the tender, passionate, undying love,*
> *Of one beer drunken slob for another.*
> *Irish Love Ballad*

Keep in mind that your own use of alcohol or drugs can have dire consequences, including the possible risk of spending your early morning hours worshipping the porcelain goddess or worrying about how to pay an attorney. Sometimes it's just not worth it. You will have wasted a day or more and stifled the attainment of your goals considerably. If you have work or school the next day, it will be important that you be alert enough to be able to function normally or to grab those "golden" opportunities that can slip by. The bottom line is to make good decisions in your social life.

Time for bed … You have a busy day tomorrow …

Care about yourself and care to give your life meaning. What standards do you set for yourself? What planning have you done? What can the community around you offer to meet your goals? What are you willing to do to achieve them? Motivate and activate.

> *Vision without action is a daydream.*
> *Action without vision is a nightmare.*
> Japanese Proverb

You have to be able to plan with flexibility, avoiding illusions, and keeping it real. Your time is valuable and should not be wasted. Have a commitment towards every one of your goals. But, keep open to the blatant fact that these often need to be updated. Don't be caught in a situation where the goal or dream is no longer realistic or attainable in its present form.

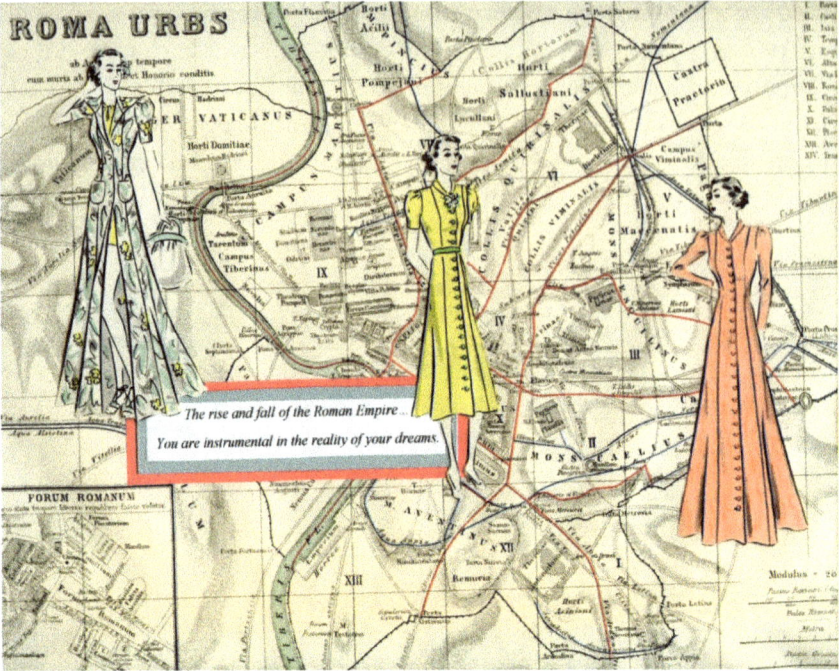

ROMA URBS

The rise and fall of the Roman Empire
You are instrumental in the reality of your dreams.

FORUM ROMANUM

Dreams are necessary to give our life purpose. Just don't lose sight of how winding that path can be. What we desire or receive in the end sometimes does not resemble the initial dream. Good dreams take both time and evolution.

Whatever you can do,
or dream you can do,
begin it.
Boldness has a genius, power, and magic in it!
W.H. Murray, 1913–1996
Scottish Mountaineer and Author

Patience is often the key to realizing our dream. It takes time to become the person you want to be and to get the things out of life that you desire. Immediate gratification can be great as long as it does not take on that thoughtless, childish form most of us loath. Great things come to those who take the time to develop realistic dreams and to establish a soundness of character.

Patience is the key to paradise.
Turkish Proverb

A person's journey or movement through life is much like the flight of a bird, and a person's character closely resembling the structure of a feather used for flight. There is a rigid shaft or rachis that provides insulation, strength, and appearance for a bird. This is much like an individual's self-acceptance, self-confidence, and what others see outwardly. Its strength is determined by how solid and reliable they prove to be.

It's the vane or blade of a feather that gives a bird the flexibility in changing height and direction. The barbule hooklets that make up each vane's branches or barbs are not great on their own, but the combined effect is sufficient to keep the feather together and allow flight. These feathers represent an individual's core values and philosophies and the essential need to adapt, to have the flexibility to change direction both mentally and physically for survival. An individual's strength in character and potential for success can be revealed by how solidly integrated and yet flexible they are maintained.

It is not the biggest, the brightest or the best that will survive,
but those who adapt the quickest.
Charles Darwin, 1809–1882
English Naturalist and Evolutionary Theorist

Breaking the Bank

Money may be the husk of many things but not the kernel.
It brings you food, but not appetite;
medicine, but not health;
acquaintance, but not friends;
servants, but not loyalty;
days of joy, but not peace or happiness.
Henrik Ibsen, 1828–1906
Norwegian Playwright

INTERESTINGLY, THE MOST frequently discussed problems encountered by young adults involve the financial arena. This is an incredibly boring and confusing subject that we just don't want to hear about or discuss—probably why we have so many problems with monetary precepts. But, perhaps if we can muster up the courage to look through some of the issues surrounding money, we won't be as likely to repeat those same mistakes in the future.

If a person gets his attitude toward money straight,
it will help straighten out almost every other area in his life.
Billy Graham, 1918–
American Evangelical Christian Evangelist

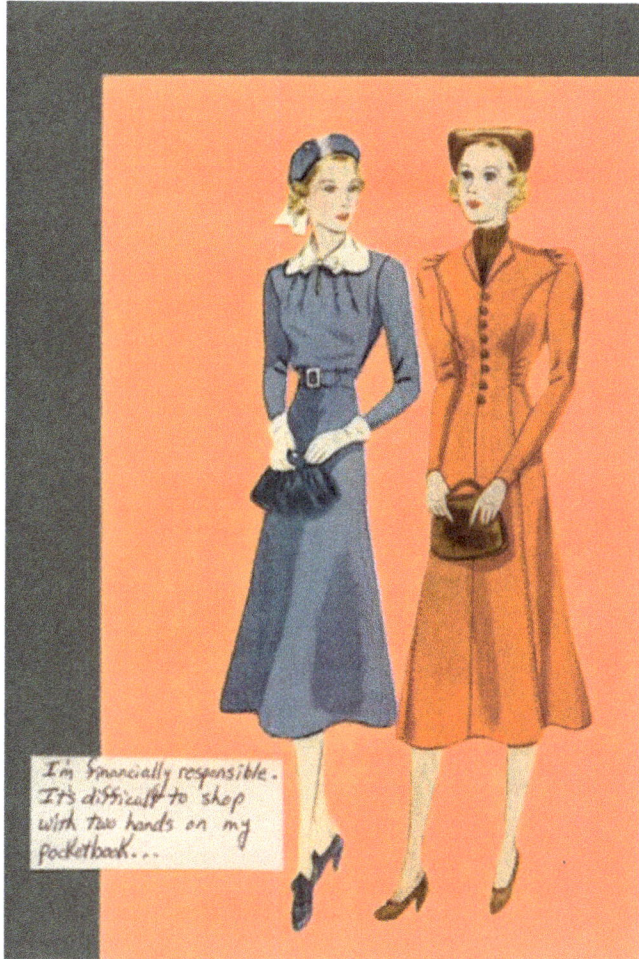

I'm financially responsible.
It's difficult to shop
with two hands on my
pocketbook...

The consensus is that so many of us don't have a thorough grasp on the requirements or obligations of living expenses, paying bills, having credit cards, or managing bank accounts. I have yet to meet anyone who has not had a tremendously difficult and/or expensive learning curve within one or more of these areas.

A fool and his money are soon parted.
Thomas Tusser, 1524–1580
English Farmer and Poet

Did you know that a budget is a list of expenses anticipated throughout an entire years' time? It also takes into account the exact amount of income (after taxes) during that same time period. It doesn't matter how much money you make, you still need to know how to manage it. You could have money to burn or very little. It's always a good idea to know what you need, where it goes, and how to make it grow.

Keep what you sow...

Money is power, freedom, a cushion, the root of all evil, the sum of blessings.
Carl Sandburg, 1878–1967
Pulitzer Prize-Winning American Author and Editor

The key to having money is to stay within a budget. Even the smallest expense needs to be calculated within your monthly requirements. If you fail to include any expense, you will probably come up short for the month. How many of us do fall short? An embarrassing number of us ignore this integral aspect of financially being able to live on our own.

My problem lies in reconciling my gross habits with my net income.
Errol Flynn, 1909–1959
Australian Actor

A good start is to make a checklist that reflects the monthly expenses and needs, including those that are irregular. The total amount will be the money required to live on each month. Making this list will also help to determine where you can cut expenses and what monies you really need to live on and the things that you really need to have. Do you have better than just an "idea or hope" of this required amount? Can you afford to live on your own or are you going to need a reliable roommate?

The art of living easily as to money
is to pitch your scale of living
one degree below your means.
Sir Henry Taylor, 1800–1886
English Writer and Editor

Padding or cushioning your budget will always help to cover those surprise expenses. You will never know when you may have an unplanned medical or auto repair bill. Or maybe your friends decided to go to the lake for the weekend. Plan for the unplanned. You will never be sorry.

The idea of having unplanned expenses naturally leads us to the difficult and intricate subject of credit …

Credit is a system whereby a person who can't pay
gets another person who can't pay
to guarantee that he can pay.
Charles Dickens, 1812–1870
English Novelist

What is a credit rating and why is it so important? Basically, it is the credit history of an individual's borrowing and repaying. It is established through car loans, credit cards, service accounts like electric bills and such. In having accounts with companies, the underlying agreement is that you will pay them what you owe. Ratings make a blatant statement about your reputation and character: that you are organized and honorable. They become more and more important as you get older. In the long run, it will enable you to purchase a home or other big ticket items. You may not be thinking of this now, but time passes quickly. It's always wise to plan ahead for the future and to protect your credit.

Credit is like a looking-glass,
which when once sullied by a breath,
may be wiped clear again;
but if once cracked can never be repaired.
Sir Walter Scott, 1771–1832
Scottish Historical Novelist, Playwright, and Poet

Many factors will affect your credit rating. The payment histories of various loans and credit cards are primary factors. Late or missing payments, or below minimums, will usually be reported to the credit bureaus if they reoccur within a short period of time. Some companies immediately report these if you have very little history with them. Others do it just as a general rule. This reporting serves as an alert message to other companies with whom you currently do business or plan to in the future. Nothing reduces a credit rating and blemishes one's character faster than not paying your bills or not paying them on time. It also creates stress for you and redirects part of your focus away from achieving your goals.

I'm living so far beyond my income
that we may almost be said to be living apart.
e.e. cummings, 1894–1962
American Author, Painter, and Playwright

Frequently individuals are initially denied credit because they don't have any. Absolutely everyone begins life with no credit rating. It's almost as though one must figure out how to go into debt to create a credit history to get credit, which creates more debt. An oxymoron all of us experience. Establishing a credit history obviously takes some time, but you can eventually achieve it via a winding path. Just remember, many of us have failed to recognize that it can take just one bad action to destroy it. Once the damage is done, it takes several years to rebuild it.

> *The surest way to establish your credit is to work*
> *yourself into the position of not needing any.*
> *Maurice Switzer, 1871–1929*
> *American Artist*

Always paying in cash never establishes a credit history. Moving around a lot or changing jobs will raise many questions. Why is it that you change residences or jobs so often? Do you have difficulty holding a job? Some companies find this a risky sort of person with whom they do not want to do business.

If you are denied a loan or credit card, always ask why. They must tell you. Check your credit reports. These are very important to review if you are denied a credit card or a loan. It is a good idea to do this annually anyway. You will be able to see who also has requested a peek at them. Lenders, creditors, insurers, service companies, and even employers can take a look at your reports. Keeping an eye on your credit reports also may help you spot identity fraud or errors. You are permitted to correct any inaccurate or incomplete information that you find in the reports. It could be that you will be denied a loan or credit card based on an error in them.

> *No man's credit is ever as good as his money.*
> *Edgar Watson Howe, 1853–1937*
> *American Novelist and Editor*

Identity theft is increasingly becoming more of a problem with the advances in technology today. Know what information is in your credit reports to protect yourself. You should never find all of your private information such as social security number, your birth date, your mother's maiden name, passport or driver's license numbers, and any whole financial account numbers (usually bank account, debit card, credit card, and PINs) together on any document, computer, or easily accessed location outside of your direct control. You do not have to have your wallet stolen to be at risk.

Credit cards can be a huge problem. Most of us don't read the fine print when applying for them. There are so many different types of cards that offer very tempting incentives such as low interest rates, rebates or cash back, special student packages, and airline points to name but a few.

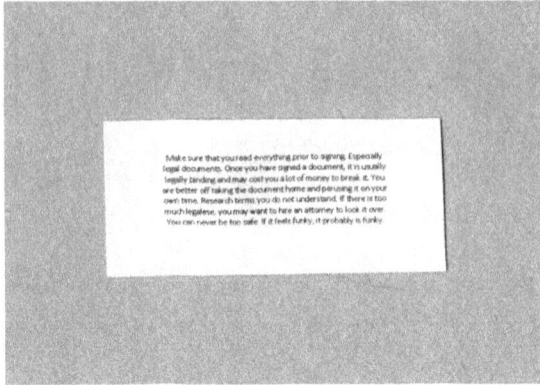

If it requires a magnifying glass or dictionary, take it home ...

What is confusing for most of us is the fine print in the agreement for the card. There are credit terms and conditions that need to be thoroughly understood. Some cards have set-up fees, program fees, participation fees, additional card fees, credit limit increase fees, cash advance fees, balance transfer fees, and fees even if no charges are made so you always have a monthly balance due. Sometimes you can ask your creditor to waive a fee, but you have to be on top of watching for this type of arrangement. It could be a onetime fee credit that suddenly reappears later.

Never spend your money before you have it.
Thomas Jefferson, 1743–1826
Diplomat and Third President of the United States

If an application or agreement is in writing and placed before you on a creditor's desk, they do expect you to read it and understand it. Never hesitate to ask questions. The best advice to follow is to thank them for their assistance and leave with the paperwork. Go home and read the information in a quiet, non-disruptive environment. Do research and gain an understanding so that you have your questions prepared if and when you go back. You will not hurt their feelings or your reputation.

It is wise to be careful in speaking with a credit card representative, especially over the phone. Sometimes there will be something that the credit card people forget to share with you. This is not always on purpose. These good people do this same job day in and day out and don't know who knows what. So it's no fault of theirs for not clarifying every detail of a card. It's their job to sell the card and the card services to you. There may be fees for some of the card services. It's your responsibility to learn and ask questions. What's the bottom line? What's it going to cost me? There are no dumb questions. Never be afraid to ask anything to completely understand what you may be getting. Credit card companies want your business. Make them work for it. Get what you want and only what you need.

Creditor. One of a tribe of savages dwelling beyond the
Financial Straits and dreaded for their desolating incursions.
Ambrose Bierce, 1842–1914
American Writer and Journalist

Apply for credit cards you are likely to get, as most inquiries by an institution are reflected in your credit report and too many can be viewed as a negative by a potential future creditor. Retail store and gas cards are easy. Better still are ones offered through where you have your bank account. Banks often have a 'secured credit card' which is issued with a limit for an amount that is deposited and guaranteed to be kept by you in an account to cover the possible expenses on the card. Educational institutions you are attending often have cards for students. They usually have lower credit lines but lower finance charges as well.

Don't apply for or carry more cards than you need. It does not provide a show-off to friends. It does not give you the look of wealth. It's the same with carrying large denominations or amounts of cash. The fact is that most businesses won't take any bills larger than a twenty. You have to realize that large wads of money can put you in real danger of being robbed. Finally, the reality is that you will come off badly to people around you, seeming reckless or becoming a target for someone who sees you as a cash cow ready for milking.

Put not your trust in money, but put your money in trust.
Oliver Wendell Holmes, 1809–1894
American Author, Physician, and Professor

Finance charges on credit cards vary. Know what the rates are and the grace periods to pay off the balance prior to being charged this amount. Usually a credit card company will allow you to request a reduced rate every six months or so. Your good payment history will be of help here. Miss a payment or go over your credit limit, good luck. Penalties are costly. And probably the finance rate and minimum payment amount will go up as a result.

You must pay at least the minimum amount due on credit cards every month. Making an early payment before you get the bill may change the due date on the card, so check on this with the bank. Yes, due dates are changeable. You can change the date on most accounts, including utilities, to make payments more in line with the day you receive your income or paycheck. Just let the company know what date you want. They will comply. It may mean that you will receive a minor bill and then a larger bill, or vice versa, to coincide with the new date. It equates to the same amount you would have paid, just split up unevenly to adjust to the new, requested due date.

Make payments allowing enough time for it to reach your account at the institution via mail or internet. Missing or late payments can be damaging for credit ratings. Late payments, less than minimum amounts due, or over the credit limit charges will result in a bank fee usually anywhere from $15 to $39. And, if a bill gets lost or payment misplaced, it is still your responsibility to recognize that it did not get paid that month. The card company may report to your missed payment to the credit agencies, and then you will be stuck writing a 'letter of excuse' for every loan you attempt to obtain for the next seven years. That's usually how long a deficient credit item remains on your record.

The creditor hath a better memory than the debtor.
James Howell, 1594–1666
Anglo-Welsh Historian and Writer

Most credit cards offer the option of using it for cash advances as well as for credit purchases. This choice has given so many of us a very painful learning experience. A horrible problem occurs when using credit cards for getting cash. The interest rate on this 'loan' is usually close to twenty percent or more! This rate is substantially more than for actual services or item purchases. Double in most cases. Additionally, your payments on the card usually go towards your charged purchases first. Once these are paid off entirely, <u>only then</u> any payments made towards the card balance will go towards the cash advance. This makes paying off the card a much longer, more expensive ordeal. The result is that the credit card company will love you …, but not enough to be your friend. Business is business.

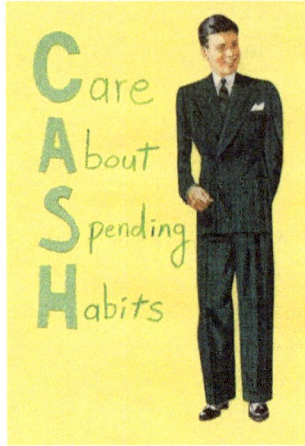

A bank is a place that will lend you money
if you can prove that you don't need it.
Bob Hope, 1903–2003
American Comedian and Actor

A credit card is a loan and not free money! You will usually pay to borrow that money. Also, a credit limit does not mean you have <u>that</u> amount of money to spend. Remember your budget? Avoid reaching the credit limit. You never know when you may need it for a true emergency situation. Leave yourself a buffer zone.

A bank is a place where they lend you an umbrella in fair weather
and ask for it back when it begins to rain.
Robert Frost, 1874–1963
American Poet

Monthly charges do add up. Keep track of your expenses. It's easy to charge a little here, a little there. It can accumulate fast. A ledger book or computer money management program can help you to visualize and keep track of your spending.

Always borrow money from a pessimist,
he doesn't expect to be paid back.
Author Unknown

Don't give access to your cards to anyone! Don't give out credit card numbers to anyone over the phone or internet unless you have initiated the contact or transaction. But be careful even then. Some repeat businesses will only need last 4 digits. Never give out any PIN numbers or use ones that are easy to figure out. Birth dates, addresses, a lost or stolen wallet, or dishonest acquaintance can make you easy pickings, so use an obscure number that only you know.

Lost or stolen cards can be a problem. If you notify the credit card company before any charges appear, you are typically not legally responsible for any charges made by the perpetrator. However, on some cards, if after charges appear and you fail to notify them promptly, you may be responsible for a portion of the expenses. It's a good idea to ask the company prior to applying for the card. They usually will expect you to indicate the disputed charges in writing with a signature sent to them.

If you do experience a missing card and call the company to report it, you will often be asked about your last charge on the card. Be prepared. They will immediately void the old card and issue a new card, which will arrive later in the mail. This means you will be without a card for a time.

Protect yourself and be sure to keep your receipts to compare with the statement when it arrives. Never just throw away receipts if the entire account number and/or signature are on it. Destroy them after verifying the charge on your statement.

Sweetie, Can we go 'dutch' tonight? My dad took away my credit card …

You may be lucky and have access to a parent's card. Follow the rules they set for using it. Respect it. Your friends and family will respect you in return. Don't ruin their credit or put a strain on their budget with irresponsible spending.

> *Life was a lot simpler when what we honored was*
> *father and mother rather than all major credit cards.*
> *Robert Orben, 1927–*
> *American Magician and Comedic Writer*

A bank account does not establish a credit history, but shows that you have money and how you manage it. Make your life easy and use a notebook or computer program to keep track of your expenses, payments, and such. It will also make you more alert to identify missing bills or account debits that are not yours.

Keep track of your expenses.

Bank account numbers are often required on credit card/loan applications. Never overdraw your accounts as it looks bad on a credit history report and will add additional fees that you will have to pay back. Most banks require a minimum balance to be maintained to avoid fees. Again, do not give anyone access to your accounts. It can't be said enough, don't be naive with PIN numbers and passwords.

What do you mean I have no money?
I still have checks!

Just because you have checks, does not mean you have money! If you run out of checks, you still are required to pay your bills. Be sure to turn in the reorder slip when you get to it in the box (usually attached to the second to last set of check pads in the box) and review the information first in case you have moved or other things have changed. You don't need those fancy checks—ask if they have free ones! But, if you just have to have the fancy checks, remember to deduct the expense on your check register and plan for it in your budget.

There's so little money in my bank account, my scenic checks show a ghetto.
Phyllis Diller, 1917–
American Comedienne and Actress

The balance the bank has for your account is based on cleared checks. They do not have any idea of what checks you have written that are still outstanding. So it's a bad idea to base your balance solely on what the bank says. Keep up with recording expenses in the check register and balancing it against your bank statements to maintain awareness of your financial well-being.

A bank book makes good reading—better than some novels.
Harry Lauder, 1870–1950
Scottish Entertainer

The consequences can be problematic if you fail to heed the rules of proper check writing. Write legibly! Always write payment checks in pen and never sign a blank check. Never postdate a check, as this is illegal, unless you know the payee and have agreed upon this. Place the written script amount on the check as far to the left as possible to avoid allowing someone else to write in a number in front of that amount. Fraud happens. This script is the usually the amount honored by the bank, not the Arabic numerals written on the right. It's a good idea to make sure they match anyway.

The same care should be taken with the name of who you are paying. The script should be to the far left to avoid writing in additional words. Write legibly to be sure your billing account is properly credited. Part of an account number or identifying invoice number should be written in the memo line of check; credit cards need only the last four digits. This is done in case the check gets separated from the payment slip, as the company will have a better chance of identifying which account to credit with the payment. Don't forget to record all of the information in your check register.

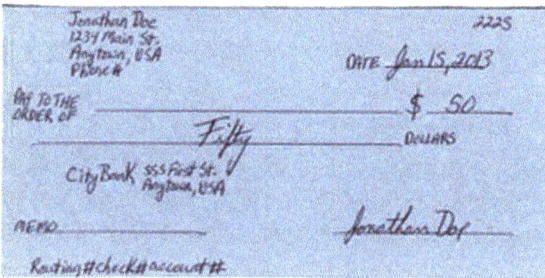

What the check looked like when you handed it over for payment...

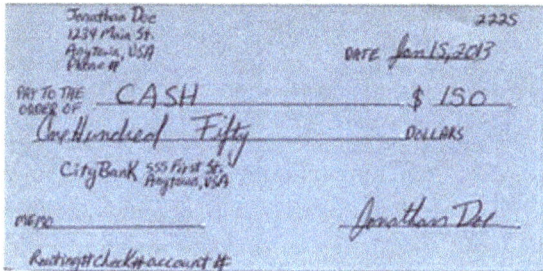

What it looked like when it arrived to the bank for cashing...
Fill in checks completely and correctly.

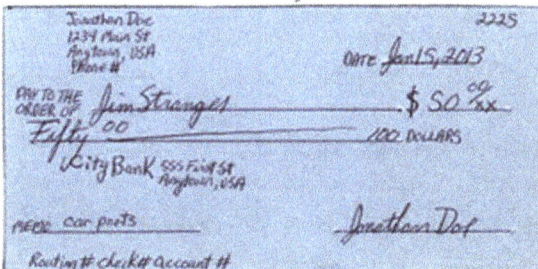

Use your own bank's branches when getting cash from an ATM. The fees can add up quickly otherwise. Most businesses will take a debit card for purchases. Some will consider it a credit card, but the money is usually still deducted from your account the same way as a check purchase. Most grocery stores will give cash back with no fees when you pay for groceries using a debit card. Again, don't forget to record these in the check register.

The mint makes it first, it is up to you to make it last.
Evan Esar, 1899–1995
American Humorist

It is a bad idea to cash checks for anyone. This includes your friends. It can take a few days for a check to clear. If it does not clear their account for any reason, the money comes directly out of your account, including any fees for the bounced check. Always politely decline any such request—there is never any reason a person should ask you to do this. They are responsible for keeping on top of their own expense needs without dragging you into it.

Deposits made at an ATM can be risky. You are much better off going to an actual bank teller. Sometimes you may be told that there will be a hold on the monies deposited. This is usually based upon where the check came from and whether you have money in the account to cover it if it should bounce. It is a great benefit if you have developed a relationship with the bank personnel. If you have been a steady and polite customer, they will usually help you out in many situations, including the immediate clearing of the deposit so you can pay bills.

Savings accounts can be set up through a bank, credit union, or an investment account. Put away money for the inevitable rainy day. Investments can be in the form of a savings or money market account, Certificate of Deposit, or investment brokerage account. Save what you can, but don't trap yourself by not being able to get to the money should it become necessary.

If you would be wealthy, think of saving as well as getting.
Benjamin Franklin, 1706–1790
American Author, Diplomat, Inventor, Physicist, and Politician

Feed me!

Rental vs. Purchase

RENTAL AGREEMENTS FOR residences, whether it involves dormitory life or apartment life, should be read thoroughly. The same principle applies when buying a residence, motor vehicle, or other big ticket item. Make sure you understand and agree with the documents completely prior to signing anything. They are binding contracts once signed, so long as you meet the legal requirements, such as age.

Residential rentals may require two months' rent up front and a security or cleaning deposit. It may seem like a lot of money, because it is. But, it can be helpful to have that last month paid for in advance should you choose to move at the end of the lease and need monies for securing the new place.

You can ask to have the second month and/or cleaning deposit spread out over a few months to make it easier on your monthly budget. You will usually get most of the security or cleaning deposit back after moving out if you leave the site as it was when you moved into it. This is all the more motivation to take care of the place, even if you don't own it. Take photographs before, during, and after you move in. You basically own most of the deposit unless your actions or inactions, or that of your friends, change it. Sometimes a cleaning deposit is not refundable because the landlord actually uses it to prepare for the next tenant. It should be written in the contract if this is the case. Know the terms of any contract.

Clean on a regular basis and you won't feel overwhelmed later.

Look up the law for your state to see how long the landlord may have to get any deposit back to you after you vacate the premises. Make sure it appears in the contract, as this may be a financial strain when moving into your next rental.

Loan contracts for car, house, and other big ticket purchases have differing interest rates available. Sometimes there are penalties for early payoffs. Read and understand the fine print. You are not stupid for asking questions. It can never be said enough that you should clearly understand what you may be signing. Educating yourself in advance will often ease the situation of reading lengthy documents containing all of that typical legalese. You will look serious and prepared if you arrive with notes outlining what you may need to know and questions you want to be sure to ask.

Borrowing is not much better than begging;
just as lending with interest is not much better than stealing.
Doris Lessing, 1919–
Persian Born, African Raised, British Nobel Prize-winning Author

Consider carefully before co-borrowing or co-signing with friends and you'll keep those friends. Have a realistic understanding of the consequences. There is a potential for personal financial ruin. Know well with whom you are signing any contract.

I can commit to the contract,
just not my roommate …

Home Sweet Home

YOU'RE MOVING INTO your own place! What a fantastic time for self-discovery. Now your new role in society will start to take shape. It is the beginning of your future. There is a lot to do in preparation for going out on your own. Make a list and refer to it often.

Pandemonium: a scene or place of wild disorder, noise, or confusion.
Dante Alighieri, 1265–1321
Italian Writer, Poet, and Philosopher

Don't forget to change your address with the post office. There is a start date on the postal notice, so this should be done a couple of weeks in advance to avoid missing important mail. You can often make the changes online. It is helpful to the postal worker if you put a note in the mailbox indicating the names of the residents and a move-in date. Do the same for the residence you are leaving.

Make sure you notify all businesses, periodicals, etc. of your address change. Use your budget checklist to identify any bills that may lag behind. This is a very common situation. You can always call a company to find out if and when the bill is due and how to go about paying it.

Change all of the locks on the residence prior to moving in. It will be your responsibility on a home you purchase. Landlords will usually pay for this on a rental. The only requirement on a rental is that you need to provide the landlord with their own copy of the key. Don't worry about this as they must give you at least 24 hours' notice prior to ever entering your space with that key. Sometimes it's longer. Make sure that this notice clearly appears in your lease. It can be embarrassing to have them show up unexpectedly. They may only be required to leave a phone message … So check your messages!

Prior to moving into your new pad, you will need to set up utilities. Some will need a week to get you going. Plan for this. Ask for exactly what services you will be receiving and what every single charge to expect on the first bill and every month thereafter. Write down everything you discuss with each company, so you will not be surprised by hidden charges for setup and the like. Include the current date and name of the employee in your notes. This helps enormously should you need to re-contact them for this or any other issue in the future. Details will save you time and trouble.

Chaos often breeds life where order breeds habit.
Henry Books Adams, 1838–1918
American Historian

Without a credit history, some businesses will require a deposit to set up a service account. It is usually refundable after a year. Be sure to record this information to keep in your files, as it will usually need to be requested by you either over the phone or in writing. Companies will not suddenly realize they owe you money and rush to get it back to you. Put it in your calendar to ask for it. You may be able to ask for it to be applied to your next month's bill. Record this request in your files so you don't forget if the bill arrives unadjusted.

Paying your monthly utility bills is required. Yes, most companies somehow manage to find you. If they don't, chances are you will be left in the dark at night or using your neighbor's hose for showers. Either way, your credit will be damaged, and you will pay a penalty fee for reinstatement of the service.

It is wise to check your mail often and to create a list of all payments that you make with typical due dates. Most will be monthly, and others could be less frequent—don't forget about these. This list will assist you in identifying any expected but missing bills before it becomes a huge or expensive problem. Refer to this list every month.

Have a set location that you keep your incoming bills. It's also good to have a set time to pay them. Some people do them immediately and others do it once or twice a month. Whatever you decide should become a set routine to keep your sanity and your accounts current. Again, be sure that payments from you will arrive at the businesses prior to the due date to ensure uninterrupted service and to avoid additional fees.

If you think nobody cares if you're alive,
try missing a couple of car payments.
Earl Wilson, 1934–2005
American Baseball Pitcher

Roommates face four major issues that should be addressed prior to sharing a residence: money, house rules, groceries, and maintenance. If you are going to have a roommate, decide up front what payment responsibilities they will have. How will utilities be paid and the lease be written and signed? Who will make sure the required monthly payments are made? What will you do to enforce agreements? Should they be in writing or witnessed by a notary? Perhaps a flat monthly charge would work for everyone?

There are crucial matters for consideration when having roommates. Will there be agreed upon house rules? When is it party time? Are there certain people you don't want over to the place? Is there a study hour? When do you both sleep? Are there medical issues you need to know about? What prescriptions do they take? What about having and maintaining pets? Can you have study groups or co-workers come over? Is this person courteous towards you and others? Do they have bad habits or temperament problems? Are there any restrictive community rules (CC&R's)? What about parking? Consider carefully about the issues all of you think are important to address before signing contracts and having roommates.

You never know how many friends you have
until you rent a house on the beach.
Author Unknown

Groceries! Roommates are notorious for using what you buy and friends love free food. Try charging for sodas and snacks. Having designated shelves in the refrigerator and cupboards does not always work. But it's a start. Who does the dishes once the food is consumed? Do you plan meals together, take turns, or each do your own thing? It's definitely much less expensive to eat as a group at home rather than going out. Just food for thought ...

Everyone knows his part, but is ignorant of its meaning in the play.
Will Durant, 1885–1981
American Educator, Historian, and Philosopher

Residential care and maintenance can be costly if not dealt with properly. Thinking about what you and roommates do at home can save you time, trouble, and cash. Always be wary about cost savings and safety.

A running toilet can raise your water bill. Leaving lights on or leaving the air conditioner on high when not home will add to the electric bill. A bad light fixture can burn down the house. An appliance left on can do the same thing. Hair irons are notorious for this.

Most of us learn about garbage the nasty way. Animals love to knock cans over and eat the contents. This problem is not limited to household pets. Raccoons, for example, can be a problem. Not only does this type of incident cause a gross mess to clean up, but it can also make your own house pet very ill. This can cost you money. Routinely take out the garbage. This means more than once a month! Perhaps it's worth investing in no-spill and secure type cans inside and out.

Housework can't kill you, but why take a chance.
Phyllis Diller, 1917–
American Actress and Comedian

Did you know that celery, corn husks, and potato peelings will stop up many garbage disposal immediately? Most of us have learned after the act. The end result is a lot of work, and sometimes a plumber, which means out of pocket money due to your error.

When you sign a lease, check to see if the landlord covers maintenance or whether there is a phone number to call. Always ask about their policy on repairs. Will you get reimbursed for repairs you have made? Some landlords will permit you to apply the cost of repairs towards the rent. Ask them before you sign the lease. What happens if you are the cause requiring the repairs? You can usually count on paying the bill if this is the case.

It's the law to provide a habitable household if you are renting. It's very important that you always do a written walk through prior to moving in. You do not want to be charged for someone else's damage. This document should be signed by all individuals involved, including every roommate and the landlord. Photographs of the rooms prior to moving in and after moving out are a valuable idea.

Rockin' the 22's

The automobile changed our dress, manners, social customs,
vacation habits, the shape of our cities, consumer purchasing patterns,
common tastes and positions in intercourse.
John Keats, 1795–1821
English Romantic Poet

OWNING A VEHICLE can give a person an incredible feeling of independence. Some equate it with an adult achievement that defines a status in society. Regardless of how you will define it, ownership always comes with a great responsibility.

Auto maintenance is frequently overlooked. Motor vehicles need gas, air in the tires, oil changes, and routine maintenance. Forgetting any one of these can be most inconvenient and costly. You may be better off to take your vehicle to an authorized service center rather than to think you are saving money letting a well-meaning friend handle repairs and maintenance. Warranty is the key issue. If it's done incorrectly, you have little recourse with no written guarantee on the work.

A driver is a king on a vinyl bucket-seat throne,
changing direction with the turn of a wheel,
changing the climate with a flick of the button,
changing the music with the switch of a dial.
Andrew H. Malcolm, 1944–
American Journalist, Author, and Columnist

Know the rules of the road! They weren't made up because some bureaucrat was bored at the office one day. Keeping the public safe and traffic flowing smoothly is the reason for such laws.

Man drives,
but the Creator holds the reins.
Jewish Proverb

Turn signals—what a great idea! Use them not so you know where you are going, but so that others might have a clue of your intentions.

Headlights use this same principle of not only allowing you to see, but that others might notice you as well, especially at dusk. It's not just a visual acuity test. You will be more aware should a pedestrian or dark vehicle pop out from a drive-way, parking lot, or unexpected place. Just consider that the dark vehicle may be you. Let other people see you.

Leave space between you and the cars around you. Know where the other cars are located. You never know when you may need to brake hard or move over quickly. Offensive and defensive actions are not just for sporting games.

A tree never hits an automobile except in self-defense.
American Proverb

If your car breaks down, you get pulled over by a police officer, or for whatever reason and you are not able to get off the roadway to a safe place, it's best to park and get out. Always wait a good distance away from the vehicle for your rescue or ticket. A police officer will usually tell you to do so depending on the particular roadway. Time and time again, other vehicles will run into the back of parked cars at the side of the road. Whether it's the brake lights or flashers, it isn't certain as to why this happens so frequently. The odds are weirdly high that the car will be struck from behind. Don't be in it or stand too close.

You know, somebody actually complimented me on my driving today.
They left a little note on the windscreen,
it said 'Parking Fine.'
Tommy Cooper, 1921–1984
British Comedian and Magician

Never drive in another vehicle's blind spot. Why? Perhaps it's called 'blind' for a reason … Be conscious of where this is on vehicles you find yourself near as well as your own. A driver should always be prepared to change lanes quickly should the need arise to move out of harm's way.

When I die, I want to die like my grandfather –
who died peacefully in his sleep.
Not screaming like all the passengers in his car.
Author Unknown

Play your music for self-enjoyment, but show courtesy towards others. Other drivers probably do not appreciate the same tunes. Not to mention that it distracts you from the task of driving safely. Hearing other vehicles, especially an emergency crew, is extremely important. You can be cited for playing the stereo too loud for this very reason.

One of the most frightening drivers to encounter is the one who is multi-tasking behind the wheel. Pay attention to your driving. Nobody can do it while applying make-up, reading the paper, getting friendly with a date, eating a burger, or texting a best friend. Many states have banned drivers from the use of cell phones. Unfortunately the reality of these dangers has failed to reach enough individuals.

> *I can't swim. I can't drive, either.*
> *I was going to learn to drive but then I thought,*
> *well, what if I crash into a lake?*
> *Dylan Moran, 1971–*
> *Irish Comedian, Actor, Writer, and Filmmaker*

Do the speed limit. You will still get there. Better to be a little late than extremely late waiting for a police car, tow-truck, or ambulance. Enter a race or performance driving school if you really feel the need to test your skills. You may even see me there! Can you say "eat my dust?"

Horn honking is actually a form of communication between taxi cabs in very large cities. It's like watching a dance as cab drivers in London and New York City 'toot toot' while they maneuver about the crowded streets. Yet, unless you fall into the category of taxi driver in a large city, horn honking should be reserved for those necessary times when safety is an issue. A person driving slower than you? Just consider the reasons why … They may have just come from their mother's funeral. Think before you honk. Think. Chances are, if you have that moment to think, the honking was not a safety issue, but rather your impatience. If you are in that much of a hurry, leave earlier. And wish that other driver a better day …

Have you ever noticed that anybody driving slower than you is an idiot,
and anyone going faster than you is a maniac?
George Carlin, 1937–2008
American Comedian, Author, Actor, and Social Critic

Never flip a finger. Not only do you look juvenile, but you never know when it could be someone you know. Try a friendly smile and wave as you pass. It tends to confuse the heck out of them (do they know you?), yet serves the purpose of waking them up to the task of driving.

Always wear a safety belt while in a vehicle, whether you are driving or a passenger. Riding in the bed of a truck without any safety constraints is also very dangerous. The human body, and other objects in the vehicle, will continue to move at the last speed of the vehicle should it stops abruptly. How painful do you think it would be to hit the windshield or the pavement at 40 mph?

You've Got the Looks

True beauty and a healthy self-image come from within, not from advertisers or the media. Beware of their ulterior motives...

CLOTHING ADS ARE everywhere. Buy what you really need and can afford—not what others think you need or what others have. Stick to that rule and you will find that you will be much better off financially and emotionally. Remember that vanity and jealousy are always negatives and should be left behind with your childhood. Dress for yourself, comfortably and appropriately, and you will radiate positive aspects of yourself to others.

Advertising is the art of convincing people
to spend money they don't have
for something they don't need.
Will Rogers, 1879–1935
American Actor, Writer, and Social Commentator

You don't need to shop at name brand stores to find their products. Outlets and resale clothing stores often have great finds of quality items that are also current in style. There is nothing like the thrill of finding designer brands with the manufacturer tags still on them at a fraction of the cost. Also think about trading in old clothes, purses/bags, shoes, and such instead of buying new. Focus on sales, coupons, and bargains as well.

Tacky trends such as the torn or baggy pants look, or the various pieces of underwear or straps hanging out, or even the sight of someone clearly lacking support in critical areas are nothing more than a clear statement of one's lack of good taste and self-respect. Insecure people attempt to force people to laugh at them. Then they don't have to wonder if they are …

Don't forget to wear a slip or undershirt if your clothing is sheer. Hold it up to the light to determine how well one can see through the material. It will affect how other people perceive you and can cost you a grade or career opportunity. It's important that people look you in the eye and listen to what you are saying. They don't if their thoughts are drawn to how you look.

Clothes make the man.
Naked people have little or no influence on society.
Mark Twain, 1835–1910
American Author and Lecturer

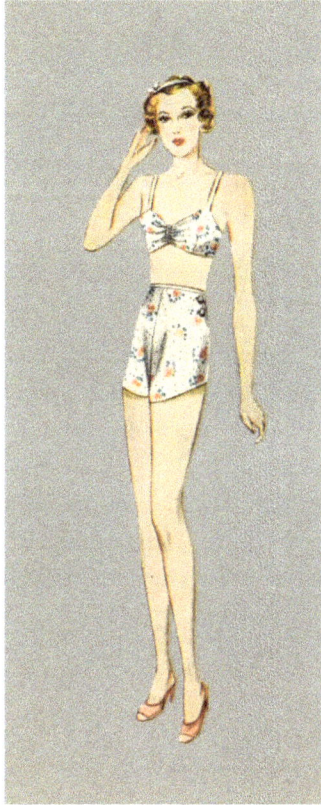

Adequately maintain and repair things you own when necessary. You have spent good money on things to make your life better. Take pride in ownership through knowing that you have only what you need and that you can appreciate what you are able to have. Respect yourself and take good care of what you have.

The happiest of people don't necessarily have the best of everything;
they just make the most of everything that comes along their way.
Author Unknown

If you have clothes that are torn or missing a button, buy a needle and thread for repairs. It's cheaper than replacing the clothing item. Sewing is not a lost art, merely something that takes practice—and a thimble.

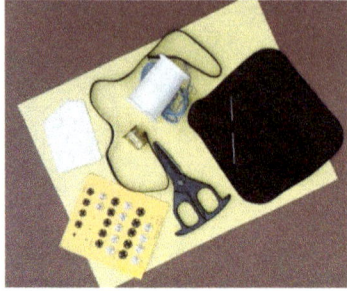

When it comes to cleaning your clothes, washers and dryers are con-venient when properly used. Read the labels on your clothing. Not sorting clothes properly for the washer often transforms whites to pink. Although with the fashion statements of today, this may not be as critical as in the past. Particular clothing items should not be put into a dryer. Again, read the labels. Remember to clean the lint trap in the dryer after each use. When unobstructed, it dries clothes much faster which saves you money. It is also a preventable cause of house fires.

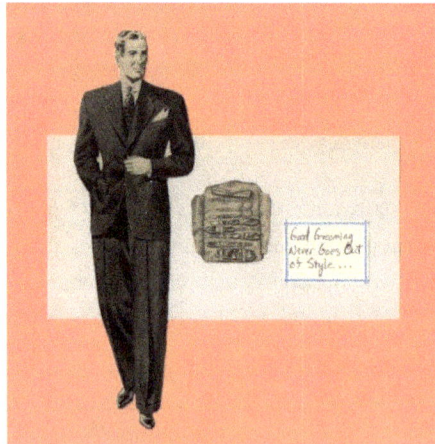

Good grooming and tasteful attire reflect positively about you. Showering may raise the water bill, but may pay off in many other ways: classroom A's, personal relationships, and job promotions. Deodorant is a must. Perfumes and make-ups should be used sparingly. In this case, more isn't always better. Usually isn't.

Keep your hair washed and styled appropriately. Always keep your teeth brushed and flossed. Do it twice a day in fact. These issues don't just concern a matter of appearance. Serious health problems can arise with improper grooming.

The bottom line is that you need to use all five of your senses when preparing to leave home. There are usually few regrets and little embarrassment in being over dressed, yet almost always in being underdressed or inappropriately groomed.

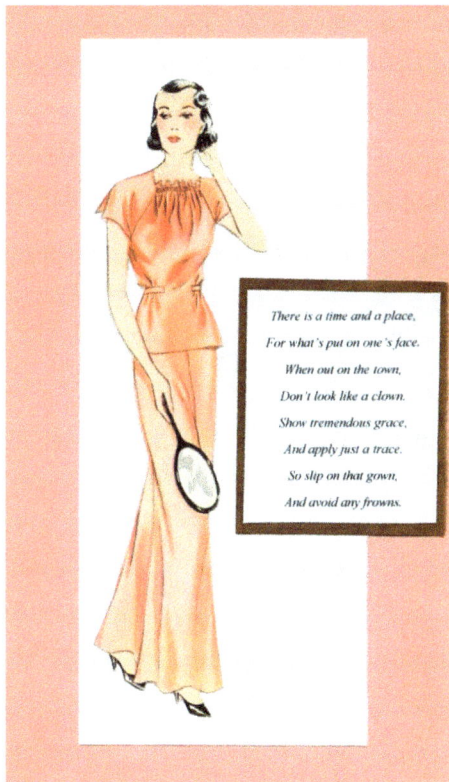

There is a time and a place,
For what's put on one's face.
When out on the town,
Don't look like a clown.
Show tremendous grace,
And apply just a trace.
So slip on that gown,
And avoid any frowns.

Beauty isn't worth thinking about;
what's important is your mind.
You don't want a fifty-dollar haircut on a fifty-cent head.
Garrison Keillor, 1942–
American Author, Humorist, and Radio Personality

Organiz-a-tion

GET ORGANIZED. SIMPLIFY and un-clutter your life. Less is really more when it comes to stuff. Save money and have only the things you really need and use frequently. Everything else is the fluff you will need to pack and shuffle here and there during the moving around that occurs during the first few years of being out on your own.

> *Our culture is superficial today, and our knowledge dangerous,*
> *because we are rich in mechanisms and poor in purposes.*
> *Will Durant, 1885–1981*
> *American Educator, Historian, and Philosopher*

Write things down. Phone calls in particular. It's important that all contacts dealing with accounts, utilities, and whatever should include names, dates, and the facts discussed as you chat. You may find it easiest to write notes down directly on the bill. Retain all those notes in that specific business' file for future reference. You never know when you may need to refer to them.

> *Knowledge is power.*
> *Sir Francis Bacon, 1561–1626*
> *English Author, Scientist, Statesman, and Philosopher*

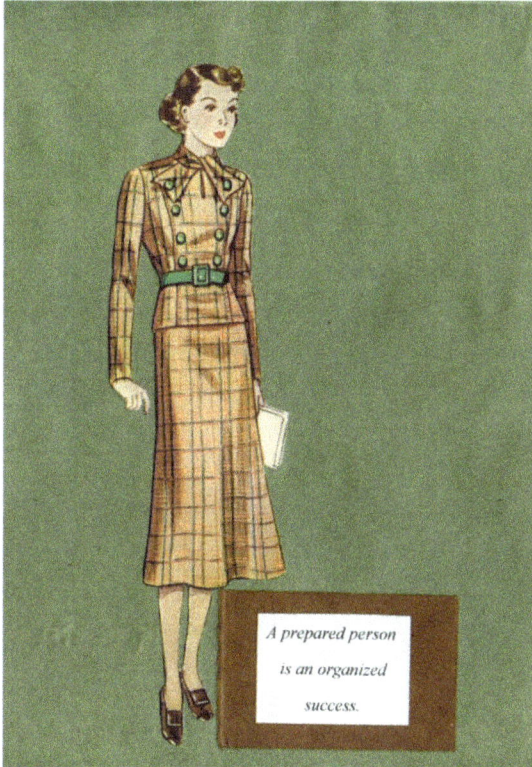

A prepared person is an organized success.

Keep important information secure. Credit card numbers should be written down with proper contact phone numbers in case they are stolen. Vehicle titles, birth certificates, social security cards, passports, and other important paperwork should be kept together. It's not a bad idea to buy a small safe or get a safety deposit box at a bank for storing these important documents.

Set up a calendar or datebook. Be knowledgeable about and maintain an active role in your commitments of time and resources. Set up an address book as well. Keep all of your contact information together and organized. This eliminates frantic searches when you need that phone number "now." Purchase some thank you notes to use once those commitments are completed ...

Make lists. Lists of what you would like to accomplish. Lists of your favorite things or places. Write out experiences you want to have. Create lists of places you would like to see someday. Lists of desires and goals are not just New Year's resolutions to be discarded a week later. Manifest your destiny by putting it out there in the universe. Making lists will facilitate in the identification of your goals; making them easier to define in clear terms of what you need to do to attain them.

If you don't know where you're going, you might not get there.
Yogi Berra, 1925–
United States Baseball Player, Coach, and Manager

How Far Ahead Have You Planned?

One on One

SOCIAL COMPETENCY IS the direct result of a healthy attitude, the use of common sense, and the development of keen observational skills. It reveals the true adult nature of who you are and how far you can go to becoming successful in the world. An individual needs to practice the proper way of dealing with people in order to gain a greater proficiency in successful and meaningful social interactions. Opportunities arise and doors open to those who are aware of the roles others have within society.

A little rudeness and disrespect
can elevate a meaningless interaction to a battle of wills
and add drama to an otherwise dull day.
Bill Watterson, 1958–
American Author and Cartoonist of Calvin & Hobbs Comic Strip

Be polite and courteous always, in all ways …

Everyone has an important role within society. The reality is that we all are in the service industry, helping each other in one way or another.

Consider this concept rationally and honestly and you can't help but agree that we all require other people to assist in fulfilling most of our needs. Be thankful that those individuals are there. It goes without saying that we must treat every person with respect during our interactions. They are real people, not just a title or position with the sole existence of serving you. Most of us work hard to achieve our dreams and deserve thoughtful consideration from everyone with whom we come into contact. It's important to keep poor attitudes away from any social or business encounter as there are never any benefits for anyone including yourself. Courtesy is never out of style.

You can catch more flies with honey than with vinegar.
Old American Proverb

Establishing relationships with individuals at banks, dry cleaners, grocery stores, school, work, neighbors, et cetera is always a good choice. You can build good bridges with all of your consistent contacts. Positive attitudes are remembered and will payoff in unusual ways—loans, discounts, and so very much more. Personalize your encounters. Shake the hand of someone who helps you. Read nametags and address individuals by name. You will find that they tend to be more helpful as a result. They also are more likely to remember you and not hesitate to assist you if needed in the future.

Charm is a sort of bloom on a [person.]
If you have it, you don't need to have anything else;
If you don't have it,
it doesn't much matter what else you have.
Sir James Barrie, 1860–1937
Scottish Author and Dramatist

Let me give you my card …

Handing out "calling cards" was the social norm in the 19th and 20th centuries. It is making a fast return to popularity today. Make your own personalized cards, as business cards are not appropriate in settings unrelated to your business. The cards serve a few important functions. It tells someone you care enough about them to give them your personal information. It permits more time to chat instead of writing down your data. It acts as a reminder to that person of your encounter and possibly providing a future benefit to you in some fashion.

Sometimes we forget that in reference to the physical, mental, and social circumstances of every individual in society, life is not linear but multi-dimensional. It's a spherical space of infinite size, where each of us moves about through time as we develop and change within circumstantial constraints. Therefore, you cannot rationalize any generalization that there is

someone above you and someone beneath you. Treat others as you would like
to be treated and you will rarely have problems in your interactions with others
.

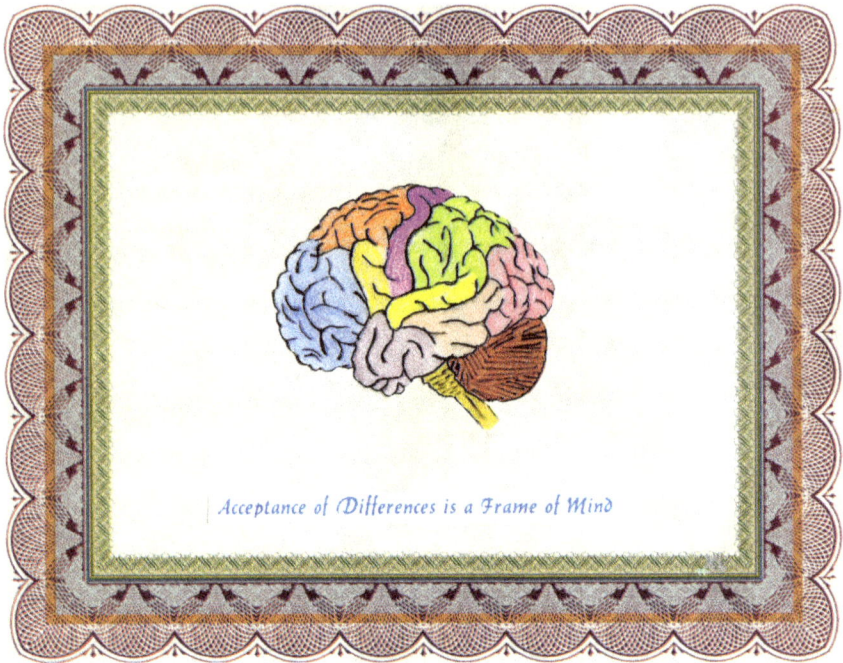

Acceptance of Differences is a Frame of Mind

Do you greet life with anticipation or expectation? It's true that our
expectations of others are sometimes tested. This may lead to irritations and
frustrations, which can draw your focus away from your goals. Set higher
standards for yourself, as you will tend to get back what you put out. At the
same time, be realistic, compassionate, and flexible. Know when to lead and
when to follow, and always set a good example. People will remember this.

> *If you want others to be happy, practice compassion.*
> *If you want to be happy, practice compassion.*
> *The 14th Dalai Lama, 1935–*
> *Nobel Peace Prize-Winning Tibetan Buddhist*

Friendships

True friendships are characterized by grace, truth, forgiveness, unselfishness, boundaries, care, and love in gigantic and mutual proportion.
Luci Swindoll, 1933–
Business Executive, Christian Speaker and Author, Musician, and Artist

LEARN HOW TO be a good friend as well as how to choose them wisely. Everyone needs to be loved and to feel a connection. Intuition and awareness of who is a real friend will develop with experience.

It is important to know and adhere to your boundaries in any relationship, whether personal or professional. These boundaries may change as a relationship evolves. Just be aware that the other person's idea of the relationship may not be the same as yours.

True friends are there for you.

Do you know the difference between a friend and an acquaintance? The level of familiarity and mutual acceptance is the foundation for defining a friendship. Being available in times of need is the sign of a true, close friend. Giving sound, un-selfish advice is another. What does it mean to you?

Sometimes being a friend means mastering the art of timing.
There is a time for silence.
A time to let go …
And a time to prepare to pick up the pieces when it's all over.
Gloria Naylor, 1950–
American Novelist

You are only as smart or successful as those with whom you associate. You will be judged by your associations. It may not sound fair or just, but admittedly it is just the way society functions. An employer or other significant person may not appreciate your friends if you run into him/ her and they behave like obnoxious, ill-mannered children. The scene will reflect badly on you. Your sense of judgment and entire character will come in to question. You could ruin a golden opportunity to achieve your dreams.

Associate yourself with men of good quality
if you esteem your own reputation;
for 'tis better to be alone than in bad company.
George Washington, 1732–1799
United States President

Know the dangers of swimming with the sharks ...

Stay away from seducers! They can take the form of the 'know it all,' constantly directing your actions because they are too afraid to do things on their own. Or they can be the 'hanger' or sidekick' to your life's activities. Neither has any real interest in your needs or your future for that matter. They have little interest in their own future ... merely living in the here and now. Not really living. Much like a babe in need of the nipple, controlling and passive friends will suck the energy and focus right out of you. Do not fall into the illusion presented by them that seduces you into fulfilling what they want. They prevent forward momentum, stalling you from identifying and meeting your own needs, and often forcing you into an unwanted role. Remember your boundaries. We have our own independent lives to lead.

Don't walk in front of me, I may not follow.
Don't walk behind me, I may not lead.
Walk beside me, and just be my friend.
Albert Camus, 1913–1960
French Algerian Author, Philosopher, and Journalist
Nobel Prize for Literature

Peer pressure, shunning, hazing, and practical jokes all should have been outgrown and left behind as an unfortunate experience of childhood. A friend worth having does not encourage you to participate in these sorts of bullying activities. There is no maturity or personal growth in such behavior. It reveals a stagnant mind. The consequences stemming from these situations will indeed tend to follow you throughout life and could seriously hinder your accomplishments and those of the victims.

Tweedledee and Tweedledum

Don't wait for approval from or time away from your friends to make choices. Chances are many of these friends will be replaced through the years. The valuable ones, who hopefully are not let go, will be behind you all the way. Maybe even beside you when they realize that you may just have something they need and value. The goal is to find a way to move into a bright independent future while maintaining good friendships.

Fill your bowl to the brim and it will spill.
Keep sharpening your knife and it will blunt.
Chase after money and security and your heart will never unclench.
Care about people's approval and you will be their prisoner.
Do your work, then step back. The only path to serenity.
Lao Tzu, 604–531 BC
Chinese Philosopher and Father of Taoism

It's best to keep relationships at work professional. But, if you develop friendships at work, leave the work talk at work and be careful with the personal stuff you share. Avoid being drawn into work conflicts on and off the job. Involvement in office politics can put a quick end to your position. This is also true of office romances. These can be a huge potential for undesirable problems. In a word: Drama.

An *absolute rule of thumb* is that you can always tell a lot about a person by how they treat animals, especially their own. Sometimes, no matter how much you care, some people are just jackasses, and this will be the moment you discover it. Too many people will agree with the accuracy of this judgment and recommend that you immediately ditch these individuals and always avoid such unconscionable people.

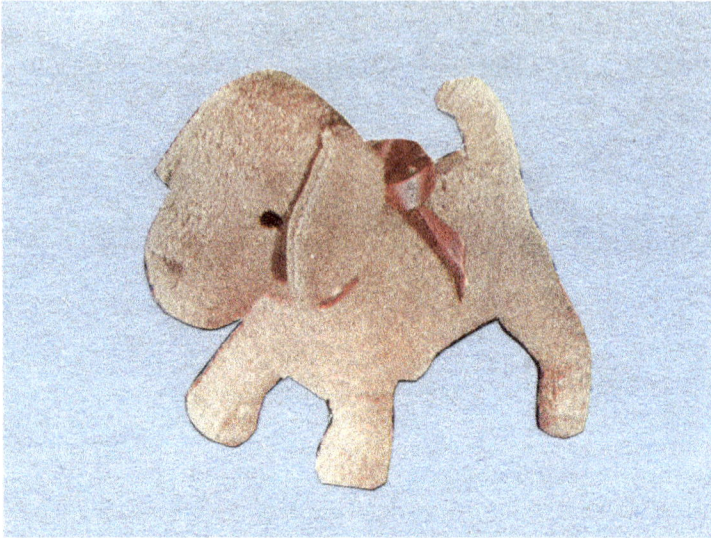

If you have men who will exclude
any of God's creatures from the shelter of compassion and pity,
you will have men who will deal likewise with their fellow men.
St. Francis of Assisi, 1181–1226
Italian Catholic Friar and Preacher

Man's Best Friend. Having a pet is a huge responsibility and can be expensive. It is usually time consuming no matter what kind of animal. These creatures are fully dependent upon you for food, shelter, and health care. All babies are babies regardless of the species. There is a huge learning or training curve to their development. That means things such as potty training, chewing, digging, climbing, vocalizations—all the behaviors that require patience and a lot of time. If you have neither, this will cost you money, and more importantly, the animal the life it deserves.

People must have renounced, it seems to me, all natural intelligence
to dare to advance that animals are but animated machines ...
It appears to me, besides, that [such people] can never have observed with attention
the character of animals, not to have distinguished among them the different voices of
need, of suffering, of joy, of pain, of love, of anger, and of all their affections.
It would be very strange that they should express so well what they could not feel.
Voltaire, 1694–1778
French Enlightenment Writer, Historian and Philosopher

Something more to consider is whether your landlord will allow you to have a pet? Are there restrictions on the type, size, or breed? Is there a special deposit they will require? Aquariums, reptiles, and pit bulls are common rejects for landlords. If one place accepts your pet, will the next? So do you then <u>abandon</u> the poor creature if you move to a new place that doesn't accept them?

If your career may require a move to a place that doesn't allow you to take this <u>dependent</u> with you, reconsider getting one. You can always get a pet later, when work and/or school make fewer demands, and you are available to properly attend to a pet's requirements of consistency, time, and especially love. Please refer to the *absolute rule of thumb* statement above. You will be judged in your human relationships based upon your choice and treatment of pets. Count on it.

We must fight against the spirit of unconscious cruelty
with which we treat the animals.
Animals suffer as much as we do.
True humanity does not allow us to impose such sufferings on them.
It is our duty to make the whole world recognize it.
Until we extend our circle of compassion to all living things,
humanity will not find peace.
Albert Schweitzer, 1875–1965
German Theologian, Philosopher, Music Scholar, and Physician

Affairs of the Heart

ROMANTIC RELATIONSHIPS CAN be nice or a nightmare. Maybe you should be asking, "Do I have to be in one right now?" Perhaps you should get to know yourself first. It's definitely a good idea to get to know the other person before committing to them at a passionate level.

Don't go for looks; they can deceive.
Don't go for wealth; even that fades away.
Go for someone who makes you smile,
because it takes only a smile to make a dark day seem bright.
Find the one that makes your heart smile.
Author Unknown

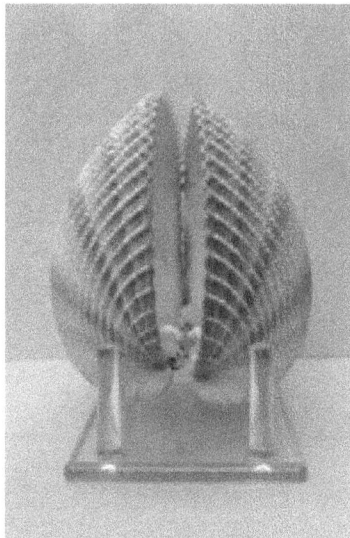

Individuals who complement one another
and fit well together enjoy good relationships.

The tendency is that people who are friends first have the best chances of having a satisfying and lasting relationship. But, remember that taking the next step from friendship to intimacy could ultimately destroy the friendship if things don't work out romantically.

A successful and satisfying relationship is one where two people can bring something back to it. You must both be able to go to work or attend classes and maintain a social network to have a healthy dating relationship. Anything affecting these activities screams probable emotional and behavioral problems that will hold one or both of you back from reaching your full potentials.

Adam and Eve by Peter Paul Rubens

Dating is an art. It's very much like an interview or character review. Decide for yourself why you either asked that individual out or why you accepted the invite. Is it serious or just for a good time? Always be respectful of them and yourself and all should go well.

A loving relationship is one in which the loved one is free to be himself –
to laugh with me, but never at me;
to cry with me, but never because of me;
to love life, to love himself, to love being loved.
Such a relationship is based upon freedom
and can never grow in a jealous heart.
Felice Leonardo "Leo" Buscaglia, 1924–1998
Professor, Author, and Motivational Speaker

When you are out with your friends for the evening, consider why you are out. Is it for a good time or to meet interesting people? Are you out for a quick pick up or a relationship? Avoid being labeled a player, a dog, loose, or whatever term is out there now. 'Someone to avoid' is ultimately what you will be labeled. Maintain your self-respect.

Word of your behavior will get out there to others. The wrong encounter could potentially destroy any future chances of meeting that one ideal person with whom you could develop a meaningful relationship. Or perhaps you will lose a good friend or acquaintance. That lost relationship could have multiple repercussions. The consequences of your actions in public can be huge. Unknown to you at the moment, a person who knows or learns of the event could be the daughter or son of a future boss with a great job for you. Or they could be the child of a professor handling your dissertation. Think of the possibilities … There is nothing like the unknown to strike you where it hurts and damage your future attainment of goals.

Clues that you need
a better pastime...
Are you a model?
Have we met before?
Do you come here
often?
What's your sign?
Who took the stars
out of the sky
and put them
in your eyes?

There are many types of intimate relationships. Some are good and others come with red flags. Who teaches us what to look for? What does a good one look like? Do we have examples in our life? What are the warning signs of a bad one? Good relationships, whether a friendship or something more romantic, require respect at all times. Additionally it must have the trust that is born from that respect.

You have nothing to lose, really, if you walk away from any questionable relationship, except the possible emotional or physical pain, discomfort, and even fear. If there is any doubt in your mind, always say goodbye immediately. It does not mean that you will never find somebody else. It is possible, and most likely, that you will find a healthier and more satisfying relationship. Patience can be very rewarding.

I just broke up with someone and the last thing she said to me was,
"You'll never find anyone like me again!"
I'm thinking, "I should hope not?
If I don't want you, why would I want someone like you?"
Larry Miller, 1953–
American Entertainer and Columnist

A controlling relationship indicates insecurity and probable lack of self-control. Everyone wants to feel secure and trusting in a relationship. There is a limit to the control of another person. Clearly there is difference between caring concern and active prevention. It can be overt and/or covert words or behaviors that will either be recognized immediately in the relationship or suddenly become apparent when the relationship is taken to a more serious commitment level.

Some "red flag" people include
the man o' war, who keeps the dangers hidden beneath the surface,
the puffer, who has self-interest and sharp barbs, and
the octopus, which uses all those arms in ways that shock us.

It is important to understand that people tend to act differently when put in different social situations. Some individuals act out only when you are alone. Friends will miss this Dr. Jekyll and Mr. Hyde behavior when not a witness to it. So don't rely on other people to tell you to get out of this type of relationship. Use your own gut feeling, even though the abuser may try and convince you to second guess yourself and other people. Pay attention to your own red flags. You are probably correct.

A beast does not know that he is a beast,
and the nearer a man gets to being a beast,
the less he knows it.
George MacDonald, 1824–1905
Scottish Author, Poet, and Christian Minister

Mental or physical attacks always signal the time to end any relationship. Hopefully you will have picked up on the signs of a bad relationship before it gets to a demonstratively abusive level. Never go back once you leave. When you break up with someone the reason you left never changes. It will always be there. This is very true in any relationship, no matter why you broke up. Be smart and know your boundaries.

Never be afraid to ask for help! Inform someone close to you if there is abuse whether emotional or physical. Talk to a friend, a parent, or adult with whom you are comfortable. Even speak to a second person to maintain your physical and mental stability. They will probably be able to help you or connect you with someone who can. Don't balk, but rather act in your own best interest. Who knows what can come of it? You could also be helping someone else in the future if a particular individual has potentially dangerous issues. But, be careful in what you say and to whom you say it.

Weigh the importance of any information you share. Protect yourself first and foremost.

Domestic violence causes far more pain than the visible marks of bruises and scars.
It is devastating to be abused by someone that you love and think loves you in return.
It is estimated that approximately 3 million incidents of domestic violence
are reported each year in the United States.
Dianne Feinstein, 1933–
United States Senator and California Politician

Don't fall into the trap of thinking that you can change someone else. If there is something about a person that you don't like or wish that they had in their repertoire, it's foolish to think that you can affect any level of change. People are free to choose who they want to be. If there is no desire to be other than what they are or how they behave or what they believe, nobody else can make this change for them. Not even a well-intentioned you. More importantly, never change who you are or what you believe for somebody else. Be true to yourself and what you need to have a fulfilling relationship. Keep looking until you find "the one."

If this works out, I promise I'll break up with my girlfriend …

If your relationship is not what you want, end it. Do not be looking for a new relationship without ending the current one. It's not fair to anyone involved and makes you look insecure and replete with commitment and integrity issues. After all, if a person is trolling for the next relationship while still involved in a current relationship, they will most likely be repeating it within the next relationship. It is best to avoid people who do this as it is definitely not adult behavior.

If you do end a relationship, it is always smart to not speak badly about others. This includes all former friends, dates, steadies, <u>and</u> their friends and families. Ask yourself what is the need to do this? In basic terminology, it's called 'badmouthing.' Sometimes it gets back to that person or others and leaves numerous relationships strained if not destroyed. Even if it doesn't get back directly to the victim, that person can be left wondering why they feel shunned or tiptoed around by others. It may not have been your intention, but the damage can have multiple repercussions. You look bad and the other people's character becomes questionable. Keep your relationships 'clean'—both the old and the current ones. Realize that you need to not 'blabber' so you won't cause any person undue damage. No matter what you attempt to do to correct this error, it's still out there. You may feel remorse in the future for initiating it, but can't be taken back once it's done. If you end a relationship, end it.

Sexual Relations—An Uncertain World

SEX IS A DOUBLE edge sword. It can be good or bad, safe or dangerous, with the right person or wrong, at the right time or not. Everyone has a choice, but our 'internal warning voice' is quite often ignored by either ourselves and/or a partner. There is so much to be said about thinking and waiting. Ask yourself an honest "why now, with this person, in this place, in this way?" Do you really know this person and for how long? Are you comfortable right there, right now? Any answer of "I don't know" requires a long moment of pause, reflection, and reconsideration. Be responsible and respectful to yourself and to others.

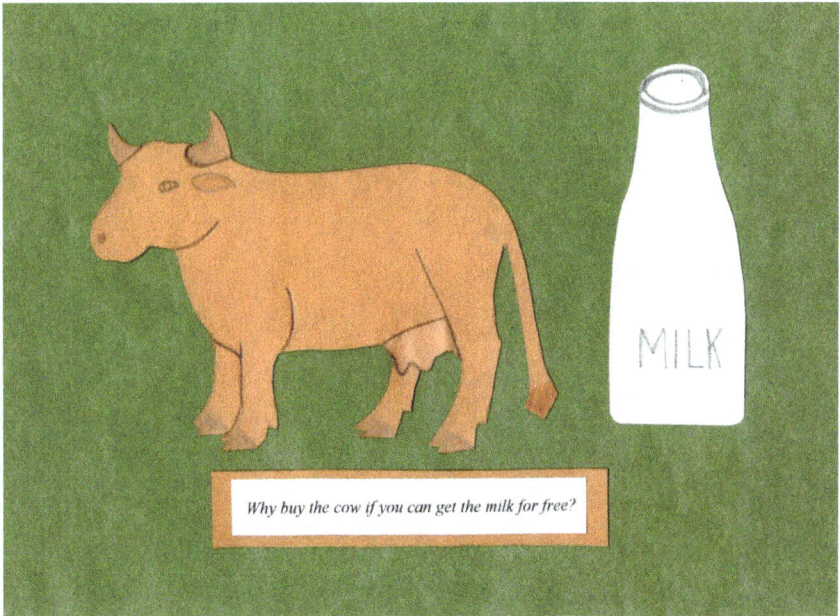

Why buy the cow if you can get the milk for free?

Be courteous to all, but intimate with few,
and let those few be well tried before you give them your confidence.
True friendship is a plant of slow growth,

and must undergo and withstand the shocks of adversity
before it is entitled to the appellation.
George Washington, 1732–1799
United States President

It is absolutely true that in having sex with that one person, you are having sex with every person with whom they have had sex, AND every person with whom each of THEM have had sex. Oral sex is still sex and just as risky for disease as intercourse. The odds of contracting a number of diseases such as, but not limited to, hepatitis B, HPV, herpes, or HIV goes up with each sexual encounter. There are approximately 25 different STD's that are transmitted through the exchange of bodily fluids. It does happen. It <u>can</u> happen to you.

It never hurts to ask your partner if they have been tested for transmittable diseases or what form of protection or birth control they are using. Defensive or evasive answers are a time to rethink the intimate moment. Get checked yourself. It's your number one health priority and sole responsibility.

I would like to see
your test results please …

What form of protection can be used against contracting these horrible and potentially fatal diseases? Most methods are not 100% perfect, because people aren't. It is disappointing that with increase in both the types of STD's and the number of individuals infected, that most people remain uneducated about the facts for each type of protection available. For example, are you aware that latex condoms break down with oil based lubricants?

If you are going to be sexually active, educate yourself thoroughly on the different forms of protection against sexually transmitted diseases. You will also need to be accepting of the fact that you may get one. Only abstinence holds the greatest guarantee against it.

There's nothing safe about sex.
There never will be.
Norman Mailer, 1923–2007
American Writer, Journalist, and Film Director

Sex often leads to reproduction. Parenthood is the toughest job on earth. Life changing in fact. Ask any parent. Are you at a place in your life right now to have children? How well do you know your partner? Are they looking to settle down and/or to have children right now? Are they looking for a way to get financial support? Do they believe in abortion or adoption? Do you? What form of contraception do you or your partner use? Have you asked? How certain are you that they are indeed being used or used properly? Do you want to marry this person? Do you like this partner enough to have regular contact with them for the next eighteen years and beyond? What damage is caused to future relationships? People you would have had a chance to date in the future might not be willing to deal with your children and the baby mama or the baby dada.

A man loses his sense of direction after four drinks;
a woman loses hers after four kisses.
Henry Louis Mencken, 1880–1956
American Journalist, Editor, and Satirist

Parenthood lasts a lifetime.

What <u>do</u> you know? Are you aware that certain contraceptives are less effective for some women who have already been pregnant? What foods, drugs, or prescriptions interfere with which forms of contraception? Are generic prescriptions as effective as brand names? Some antibiotics are known to render birth control pills ineffective. It's your body, and potentially not just your life. Be responsible and educate yourself.

There has been no ill effect proven in using more than one form of protection. For example, use a condom as well as a diaphragm or pill. But, even then there are no guarantees. It is a fact that only abstinence offers 100% pregnancy protection. It's all about self-control—controlling what you want in life to make it happen.

Parents and Family

WHEN YOU MOVE out, you may miss your parents. It could be one or both of them. You may find that you miss your siblings or extended family members. Many of us have experienced this sense of loss. It's natural to have these feelings. These individuals have been a major part of what you were used to in everyday life. For each of us, the known patterns of daily living must evolve so that we can grow through new experiences and new relationships.

Home is a place not only of strong affections,
but of entire unreserved;
it is life's undress rehearsal, its backroom, its dressing room,
from which we go forth to more careful and guarded intercourse,
leaving behind … cast-off and everyday clothing.
Harriett Beecher Stowe, 1811–1896
American Abolitionist and Author

In basic terms, the role of a parent is to define and enforce behavioral boundaries with love. Sometimes lots of it … It is the responsibility of parents to instill and exemplify healthy attitudes and emotional stability. When they send us off into the big, wide world, they experience many conflicted emotions. There is trepidation for the bad experiences and exhilaration for the good. Be patient with the changes they will deal with upon your leaving home.

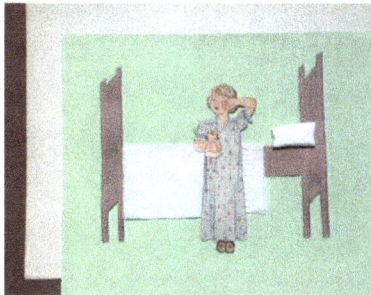

Who's going to tuck me in when I grow up?

Many of us leave home thinking that mom and dad know everything. How am I going to make it without them? Parents do the best that they can to prepare their children for the surviving on their own. Over time, with experience and maturity, we do come to the realization that our parents learned all that they needed to get themselves through events in their own lives. These were their own learning experiences which are not the same for everyone, including their own children. You will inherit a large part of what they know, and incorporate your own learning to become a unique member of society.

> *Hold your parents tenderly,*
> *for the world will seem a strange and lonely place*
> *when they are gone …*
> *Emily Dickinson, 1830–1886*
> *American Poet*

Sometimes the phone bills soar when you first move out. That's normal, just prepare financially for it. It's very important that when a family member does call, don't ignore the ringing phone. That individual is going through changes as well and may just need to hear your voice, however briefly. It's important to maintain contact with your family throughout your life. Exceptions are very rare.

Romance fails us and so do friendships,
but the relationship of parent and child,
less noisy than all the others,
remains indelible and indestructible,
the strongest relationship on earth.
Theodor Reik, 1888–1969
Psychoanalyst and Author

Parenthood is a privilege not a right. Home is supposed to be a place where we feel safe and encouraged. Unfortunately, this is not the case for everyone. Some of us may think we've had bad parents … This may be true or not. The real truth is, get over it. Know the bad or difficult points. And don't repeat them. Move on to what you want and need. This doesn't mean letting your relationship with them end. You can't just write them off or pretend they don't exist now that you have a new found freedom and independence away from daily interactions with them. Just learn to recognize when it's not working appropriately for you at the moment, especially when they are not open and supportive to your own healthy evolution.

Children are natural mimics;
they act like their parents in spite of every effort to teach them good manners.
Unknown Author

It's perfectly acceptable to take a 'time out' to let any family situation dissipate and to allow members the opportunity to learn and grow and to make changes in their own lives. You can and should always go home to see what is there from time to time, and to determine just how you currently fit into those family dynamics. It always changes. Just as all things should. And, it's possible that it could be your own issues that are/were the problem.

Parents are not perfect. They are people trying to make their way through the world just like you. The goal of parenthood is to make life better, full of possibilities for their children. But, these same children can make life difficult for parents. Be aware of and take responsibility for your own role in the family dynamics.

Siblings are experiencing a part of the same process of growth and change as you. Assure, support, and advise them in appropriate ways. They may act different after your departure, either towards you and/or within the family. Relationship dynamics always flux within families, both due to the passage of time and as a result of any member leaving or being added to the household.

Each one of us comes from a unique environment from which one is 'thrust' into from the moment of birth. But, the fact is that each of us has the "free will" for change no matter from where we come. Our background and circumstances influence who we are, but we are responsible for who we become. We could waste our lives blaming so and so, or make better use of our time by focusing on what needs to be done to make our dreams come true.

I believe the children are our future
Teach them well and let them lead the way
Show them all the beauty they possess inside
Give them a sense of pride to make it easier
Let the children's laughter remind us how we use to be.
Linda Creed, 1948–1986
Singer, Songwriter, and Lyricist

Comparative Interactions

THE ILLUSION THAT the 'grass is greener' for someone else is held by each of us at some point. The reality is that struggles exist for everyone. We all have our own issues and our own baggage that life deals out. The 'if only' scenario is an illusion only if your sights are set on someone else's backyard. Search for your own 'if only' and make it happen. Don't compare yourself to others. They may be more screwed up than you think. Remember what Kermit the Frog said, "It's not easy being green …"

Don't bother just to be better than your contemporaries or predecessors.
Try and be better than yourself.
William Faulkner, 1897–1962
Nobel Prize-winning American Author

The 'what if's' will always exist in life. Your choice is either to live for today with the goal of having a better future or to get bogged down in your past or to be envious over the lives of others. There are many paths to take every day. It is in your best interest to get good at recognizing the right ones for you.

Why do we sometimes do things uncharacteristic of our true selves? Perhaps it is because we stop thinking for ourselves. Is it laziness? Not necessarily. Sometimes it's merely what seems to be the easiest route to take. Easy is a positive word for most of us, but not very "thought-ful." And sometimes not the right decision to make. Tough is a hard word. It is pounded into us from as early as grammar school. Sometimes you just have to forge ahead and take the rough road to get to where you want to be.

Some individuals may choose the easy route to avoid personal suffering. Suffering, the Dalai Lama says, is what all living creatures have in common. It is what we do with this that makes the difference. There are two categories of suffering. There is the physical suffering we experience from injury or disease. Then there is the often discounted mental or emotional pain that comes from our experiences. Overcoming the fear that stems from whatever the source of this suffering is a challenge and a huge step towards maturity. You can do it with a healthy, positive mind set.

In order to learn the most important lessons of life,
one must each day surmount a fear.
Ralph Waldo Emerson, 1803–1882
American Writer, Poet, and Philosopher

Allow yourself to change. There is always room and time for change. Other people may have a rigid view of who you are that doesn't seem to accept change. So what? Change is good. Change is healthy. Change is a normal process of self-discovery and development. Do it anyway. If it really matters to others, then they will have to re-evaluate who you have become.

The only man I know who behaves sensibly is my tailor;
he takes my measurements anew each time he sees me.
The rest go on with their old measurements and expect me to fit them.
George Bernard Shaw, 1856–1950
Irish Playwright

Regrets are the past crippling the future.

No one can live in the past … Take with you the lessons learned, but leave the rest behind. Don't wait for the future. You exist in the here and now. Sometimes we have to take control of the right to choose how we want to exist. You must develop the self-confidence to move forward into a healthy future of your choice and your creation by choosing how you live today.

We are made wise not by the recollection of our past,
but by the responsibility for our future.
George Bernard Shaw, 1856–1950
Irish Playwright

Break the pattern

Examine your current circumstances in relation to the outside world history and in relation to your own history. History contains patterns, because people do, and history does indeed tend to repeat itself. Patterns are continually being formed in your thinking and in your behavior. These may be successful or not depending on the circumstances of the moment. Ditch those patterns that have not worked or have held you back. Move forward using those insights and skills that work for you right now, and keep yourself open to new ones that will appear over time and through experience.

> *The further backward you look, the further forward you can see.*
> *Sir Winston Churchill, 1874–1965*
> *British Politician*

There is a difference between advising, dictating, and criticizing. Examine your motives before both the giving and taking of advice. What is really trying to be accomplished? Will it improve you, the person, or the world?

> *A drunk man who smelled like beer sat down on a subway next to a priest.*
> *The man's tie was stained, his face was plastered with red lipstick, and a half-empty*
> *bottle of gin was sticking out of his torn coat pocket.*
> *He opened his newspaper and began reading.*
> *After a few minutes the man turned to the priest and asked,*
> *"Say Father, what causes arthritis?"*
> *The priest replied, "My Son, it's caused by loose living, being with cheap,*
> *wicked women, too much alcohol, contempt for your fellow man, sleeping*
> *around with prostitutes and lack of a bath."*
> *The drunk muttered in response, "Well, I'll be damned," then returned to his paper.*
> *The priest, thinking about what he had said, nudged the man and apologized. "I'm very*
> *sorry. I didn't mean to come on so strong. How long have you had arthritis?"*
> *The drunk answered, "I don't have it, Father. I was just reading*
> *here that the Pope does."*
> *MORAL: Make sure you understand the question before offering the answer.*
> *Author Unknown*

Passing judgment is a normal process in day to day living. It's what we base our decisions upon prior to speaking and acting. But, there is a difference between analytical and critical judgment. Take a look at things positively and avoid criticism. Firmly root yourself in reality, understanding that things may not be what you have always assumed.

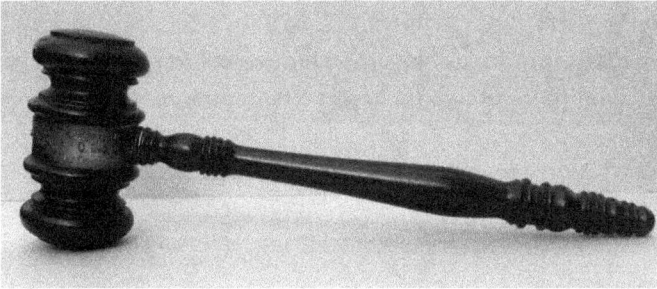

We judge ourselves by what we feel capable of doing,
while others judge us by what we have already done.
Henry Wadsworth Longfellow, 1807–1882
American Educator and Poet

Others will judge us. So what? Success is individualistic. The greatest importance lies in our becoming who we want to be. Dreams and plans we set for ourselves are the blueprint for our own measure of success. Live for one's self and one's own future and not that of others'; as they will pass onward into one of their own making. People will see you how they will, and it will not necessarily be the same. Again, so what? Let pride reign where it belongs, in your accomplishments.

Don't worry over what other people are thinking about you.
They're too busy worrying over what you are thinking about them.
Edelstein's Advice—Eponymous Law

Act in your own best interests, without harm to others'. You may have the right to be angry but not to be cruel. There are always victims and volunteers. It often doesn't seem like there's a choice, but there is. Look for the positive options in dealing with people.

Fear is the parent of cruelty.
James Froude, 1818–1894
British Historian, Writer, and Editor

Revenge is an all-consuming act. There is never a winner nor a sense of satisfaction gained from such vindictive exploits. It tends to be a self-degrading act that demonstrates a lack of self-restraint and leaving widespread repercussions in its wake. Leave the wrongs of the past behind as lessons learned. Your focus belongs in the present to become the best person you can be and thus making the world a better place.

Before you embark on a journey of revenge, dig two graves.
Confucius, 551–479 BCE
Chinese Social and Political Philosopher and Educator

Forgiveness is a difficult concept. In forgiving a person for their actions, we are really just letting go of the anger and resentment and the desire for punishment. It never means forgetting the wrong doing, merely not allowing it to consume and further devastate your life. You can choose to either walk away or waste away.

Always forgive your enemies—nothing annoys them so much.
Oscar Wilde, 1854–1900
Irish Writer and Poet

Respect yourself and others. Such a demeanor will come across in the way you present yourself in words and actions, and will come back to you tenfold. Maintain your dignity and propriety and don't be pompous. Never cause scenes in public. Self-control is an adult characteristic. Become known for the honor and integrity that comes from this self-control.

How you deal with things is the measure of one's success. You can pick the path and you can choose to excel in what you like or change direction completely to something you discover that you like better. The difficulty lies in surviving the early years and getting through the later ones with as few major detours as possible.

A smooth sea never made a skillful mariner.
English Proverb

The Weight of the World

AN INDIVIDUAL'S CHARACTER or who they are or can be-
come is made up of the combining influences of biology (mental and physical aspects), behavior (outward expression of self within specific situations),
and environment (where one has or will spend time and with whom one
interacts). Any one of these areas will take a major part in creating an individual's potentials in life. Limitations in any of these areas will result in lim-
iting one's potential.

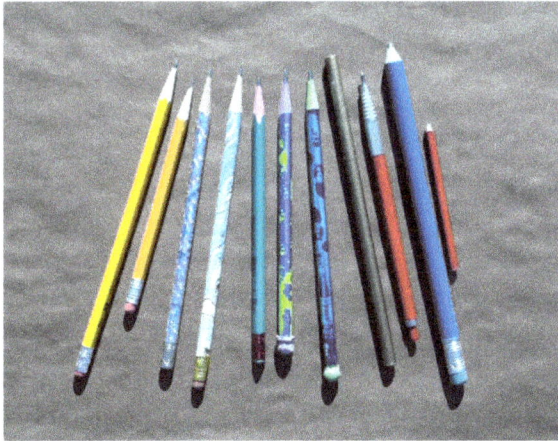

*Pencils can be thick, skinny, short, tall, different colored skins
and shells, missing integral parts, and made with modified mechanics.*

Not everyone is created physically or mentally equal. Mother Nature,
genetics, and sometimes environmental forces (such as accident or disease)
have seen to that. Additionally, our individual behaviors influence and are
influenced by the environments we encounter either routinely or by chance.
There is a tremendous variety of environments in which each of us experiences life and develop into our own unique being. This is why we have such
diversity in humanity. Truly life would be monotonous and boring other-

wise. Ultimately it will be one's ability to learn and to adapt that determines the future.

It is not the biggest, the brightest or the best that will survive,
but those who adapt the quickest.
Charles Darwin, 1809–1882
English Naturalist and Evolutionary Theorist

We can no longer say that we live in a time where it's a small, restricted neighborhood that raises us. It may start out seeming that way when we are young, immature, and vulnerable. But the world is fast becoming our back-yard. Failure arises from not accepting this. There are so many venues and opportunities available in this age of globalization not to take advantage of them with the abilities that we have.

It isn't where you come from, it's where you're going that counts.
Ella Fitzgerald, 1917–1996
American Jazz Vocalist

Each and every one of us has to take what we have and make it or change it into something we want. Our goals. Our dreams. Our responsibility. It's like a football game where most of us can now become the quarterback or the head cheerleader. And it's our own responsibility to avoid fumbling the ball or dropping the baton, because we will have to deal with the consequences. It's unfortunate that the repercussions of our actions or inactions may also touch others in ways we can only begin to imagine. Be responsible in what you do.

Mind your target …

The "greatest" lives come to those who follow the rules. They are usually the safety boundaries within which we all can survive. Some are rigid and others flexible. They have to exist in society. Without them there would be anarchy and chaos. Everyone tests these boundaries. Only the wisest realize their benefits and make adjustments to what works in the real world, or become involved in different ways to change them.

It is circumstance and proper timing
that give an action its character
and make it either good or bad.
Agesilaus II, 444–400 BC
Greek King

Living in the moment with little notice for the significance of consequences for the actions of yourself or others is not a life. Poor impulse
control is a behavior associated with emotional and cognitive immaturity.
Unfortunately this can be seen as a big part of the immortality belief that "it
can't happen to me." Usually we can find this type of expressions in teenagers. Our society is full of examples of testing the limits.

It is a fact that for every action there is a reaction. Avoid the negative
ones by carefully considering the potential consequences to your actions.
It will become easier and more automatic over time as you gain knowledge
and understanding through your own experiences and in observing
others.

Stop blaming, complaining, and whining. Take responsibility for your
actions—the good and the bad. It makes the good that much sweeter if
you acknowledge the mistakes. Admit when you make mistakes and learn
from the mistakes of others. Life is far too short to waste time ignoring
the mistakes you make yourself or learning first hand all of the lessons and
consequences that are out there. Do you need to stick your own finger in a
live electrical outlet to know that you will receive a shock or burn? Rules are
made from consequences. Learn from them and accept the ones that make
sense without the need for you testing them all.

Learn when to be serious. Learn when to laugh at yourself, especially your 'faux pas' and 'dumb' mistakes. It doesn't mean that you are a joke—just that you can recognize a behavioral mistake when you make it. It's all about being comfortable in your own skin to admit errors. Find that comfort zone with who you strive to be. People will tend to be more comfortable around you—as well as being more willing to admit their own blunders.

Maturity has more to do with the types of experiences you have and what you learn from them. If you make a mistake, be quick to make amends. Two of the most difficult things to say are "I'm sorry" and "You were right." But, it's not enough that others forgive you. It's equally important to learn to forgive yourself.

I am not bound to win, but I am bound to be true.
I am not bound to succeed,
but I am bound to live by the light that I have.
I must stand with anybody that stands right,
and stand with him while he is right,
and part with him when he goes wrong.
Abraham Lincoln, 1809–1865
16th United States President

Knowing right and wrong—that's what survival is all about. Most people have a particular set of knowledge called intuition or common sense. That primal instinct or gut feeling that lets us know when something is right or wrong. It is important to recognize it and be willing to tweak behaviors in order to survive with less strife. Sometimes this means letting go of your ego and listening to the recommendations of others. Be open to learning. The ultimate goal is success in your life and perhaps the possibility of having a positive influence on someone else's.

The Wolves Within

An old grandfather, whose grandson came to him with anger at a schoolmate who had done him an injustice, said, "Let me tell you a story. I too, at times, have felt a great hate for those that have taken so much, with no sorrow for what they do. But hate wears you down, and does not hurt your enemy. It is like taking poison and wishing your enemy would die. I have struggled with these feelings many times."

He continued, "It is as if there are two wolves inside me; one good and does no harm. He lives in harmony with all around him and does not take offense when no offense was intended. He will only fight when it is right to do so, and in the right way.

But the other wolf, ah! He is full of anger. The littlest thing will set him into a fit of temper. He fights everyone, all the time, for no reason.

He cannot think because his anger and hate are so great.

It is hard to live with these two wolves inside me,

for both of them try to dominate my spirit."
The boy looked intently into his grandfather's eyes and asked,
"Which one wins, Grandfather?"
The Grandfather solemnly said, "The one I feed."
Author Unknown

You cannot expect to continually turn to bureaucratic powers or the welfare state when you encounter something that you don't like or that you need. You can get bogged down by focusing too deeply on scapegoats and nonviable solutions. Dissatisfaction is a huge growth opportunity. Tolerance of the imperfections of situations and of others is the key to true freedom of existence. Take the responsibility of making your own life what you want it to be. If you can't tolerate an injustice, be a positive influence to change those things that could benefit society.

I do not choose to be a common man.
It is my right to be uncommon—if I can.
I seek opportunity, not security.
I do not wish to be a kept citizen, humbled and dulled by having the state look after me.
I want to take the calculated risk, to dream and to build, to fail and to succeed.
I refuse to barter incentive for a dole.
I prefer the challenges of life to the guaranteed existence,
the thrill of fulfillment to the stale calm of Utopia.
I will not trade freedom for beneficence, nor dignity for a handout.
It is my heritage to think and act for myself, enjoy the benefit of my creations,
and to face the world boldly and say, this I have done.
Dean Alfange, 1899–1989
American Statesman

Brain Washing

IN THE GENERAL population, the media has gained control of thought and discourse in society. You absolutely can't believe everything you hear or read anymore. What portion of the news is based on complete facts? Is reality television truly reality? Increasingly today's news and television programs feed us shock and sensationalism. It seems to be what sells, which is the bottom line in our capitalistic society. We are sadly becoming desensitized to what is appropriate in thought, word, and behavior.

If you don't read the newspaper you are uninformed,
if you do read the newspaper you are misinformed.
Mark Twain, 1835–1910
American Author and Lecturer

Can you read me a good story?

Read things that are interesting. Watch informative television. There are so many quality writings and television programs available. They are not difficult to identify. Doing so will stimulate the mind and provide interesting things to talk about. You may even be able to apply a thing or two to a job or class assignment. The 'reality' is that you will become a more engaging person with whom people enjoy being around.

> *A healthy male adult bore consumes*
> *each year one and a half times*
> *his own weight in other people's patience.*
> *John Updike, 1932–2009*
> *American Writer and Critic*

I swear it's true! I heard it from Stacy
who heard it from Jane, who heard it from Lisa …

Take care with what you learn and disseminate to others. Make sure your source is reliable, accurate, and accountable. Misinformation can spread like wildfire, jumping around from person to person until the truth or the complete facts are lost. Don't get caught in an embarrassing situation by providing information in an office report or school project that is not verifiable. It is possible to have your job or education plans ended by failing to take heed of this potentially painful experience. You need to be able to distinguish between the advertised story and the valid facts.

Before you speak,
ask yourself:
Is it kind?
Is it necessary?
Is it true?
Does it improve the silence?
Sri Sathya Sai Baba, 1926–2011
Indian Guru, Spiritual Leader, Philanthropist, and Educator

No two people ever see the same event the same way. There is always more than one solution or more than one way of looking at any one thing. Don't get bogged down by the endless possibilities, yet don't be inflexible by not being open to the endless possibilities. Misconceived perceptions and notions can be very damaging to yourself and others. It truly reveals a closed, immature mind.

A social worker from a big City in Massachusetts recently transferred to
the Mountains of Kentucky and was on the first tour of her new territory
when she came upon the tiniest cabin she had ever seen in her life.
Intrigued, she went up and knocked on the door ... "Anybody home?" she asked.
"Yep," came a kid's voice through the door.
"Is your father there?" asked the social worker.
"Pa? Nope, he left afore Ma came in," said the kid.

"Well, is your mother there?" persisted the social worker.
"Ma? Nope, she left just afore I got here," said the kid.
"But," protested the social worker, "are you never together as a family?"
"Sure, but not here," said the kid through the door. "This is the outhouse!"
Author Unknown

Take the time to comprehend and appreciate the diversity in humanity. Unless you have had the glorious opportunity to experience and understand other societies and cultures, their truths and realities will usually not be recognizable or understandable to you. Limited perspectives are based on limited experiences.

The golden rule of conduct is mutual toleration,
seeing that we will never all think alike and we shall always
see truth in fragment and from different points of vision.
Mohandas Karamchand Gandhi, 1869–1948
Indian Spiritual and Political Leader

Develop and maintain a reputation as a truthful person and there will be little in life that you can't accomplish. This means being thorough in telling the story of any event. Leaving out certain pertinent facts can change a story drastically. Selectively presenting facts is lying by omission or TLI (too little information.) The truth then becomes a lie. You may believe something to be a 'white lie,' but it's still a lie. It can become the definition of propaganda and is not far from becoming sabotage because the intent to manipulate and influence the audience is there.

You're never as good as everyone tells you when you win,
and you're never as bad as they say when you lose.
Lou Holtz, 1937–
American Football Coach, Author, Motivational Speaker, and Television Commentator

Sabotage is the malicious use of words and or behaviors with the deliberate intent of leading one or more individuals into a specific mode of thought and/or behaviour towards another specific individual or institution. Some individuals are slick at planting the bad seed. Others are adept at receiving and accepting such mis-information.

The choice of words or the mere raise of an eyebrow at the opportune moment conveys a message. Unfortunately that message can contain the toxins for social dis-ease. Mob mentality is a perfect example of such leading by the nose-ring. Think for yourself and decide what is just, appropriate, and real. Others may be able to plant a thought, but they can't make you chose to act upon it.

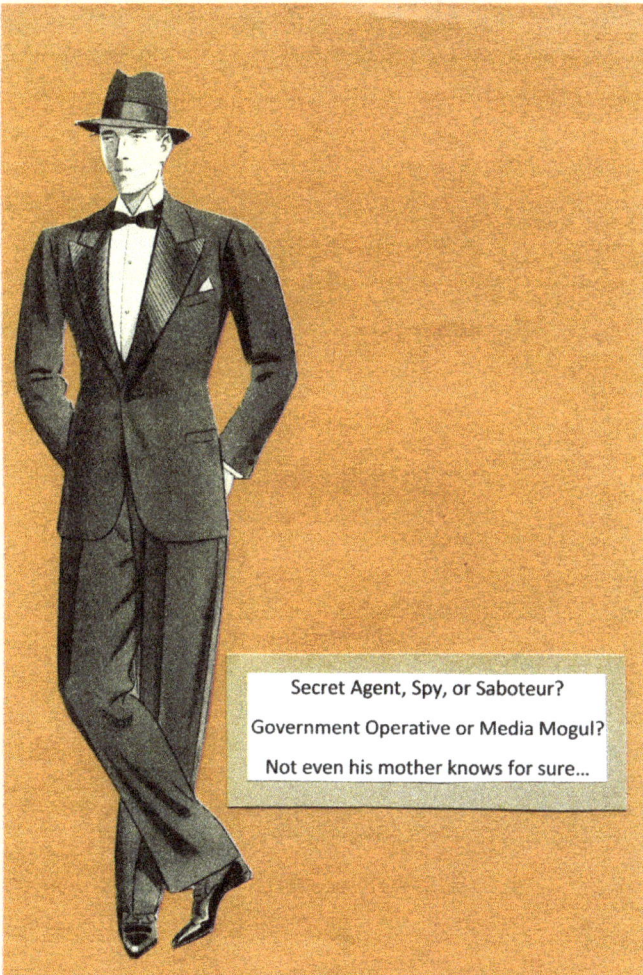

Secret Agent, Spy, or Saboteur?

Government Operative or Media Mogul?

Not even his mother knows for sure...

Attempts at brain-washing are all around us. The United States Department of Defense (DOD) actively uses and defines "perception management" as actions used to convey and/or deny selected information to an audience to influence emotions, motives, and objective reasoning, resulting in behaviors and actions favorable to the originator's objectives. It combines truth projection, operations security, cover and deception, and psychological operations. This seems a lot like the definitions for propaganda and sabotage. Unfortunately this perception management is present in our daily lives. We hear it in the news and in the speeches of people we should be able to trust. As intelligent adults, we must always remember to analyze what we see, hear, and read.

When told the reason for daylight saving time the Old Indian said,
"Only the government would believe that you could cut a foot off the top of a blanket,
sew it to the bottom, and have a longer blanket."
Unknown Author

Words and Deeds

YOUR CHOICE IN the words that you use and how they are deliv-
ered are very important. What you say and do in every situation says a lot
about your character. Character is who we are as an individual and a member
of a community.

Watch your thoughts; they become words.
Watch your words; they become actions.
Watch your actions; they become habits.
Watch your habits; they become character.
Watch your character; it becomes your destiny.
Author Unknown

Take into consideration the importance of both 'who is the audience' and 'what you are trying to communicate.' There is significance to the use of correct and essential words and proper grammar. It reveals much about your social and formal education as well as your background.

Know your audience.

The use of slang and swear words typically raises questions about your intellect, draws attention away from what you are trying to say, and may reflect some emotional instability. You will most likely lose the respect and focus of the listener. Using commonly known descriptive words, known as adjectives, will ensure that the listener understands what you are really saying.

Why do they rate a movie R for adult language?
The only people I hear using that language are teenagers.
Unknown Author

Speaking clearly exhibits a sense of confidence by the speaker and confers validity to what is being said. Mumbling reflects a sense of insecurity in the speaker, causing the audience to question what is being communicated.

You will also need to put yourself in the place of the listener by paying attention to outside noises and their personal needs: are there airplanes overhead or does the listener wear a hearing aid? Be aware and adjust yourself accordingly or risk losing the audience.

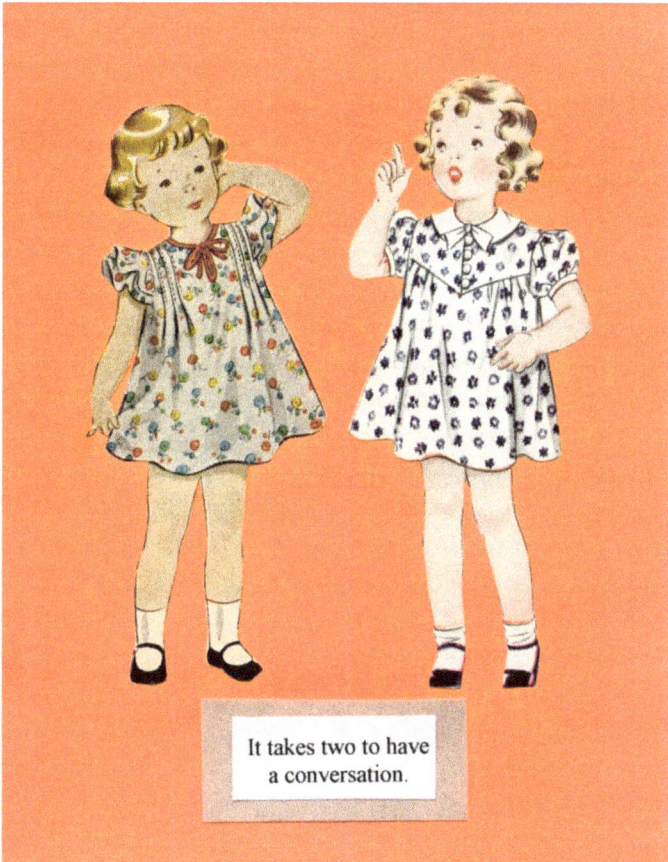

It takes two to have a conversation.

Conversation requires at least two involved people in an exchange of ideas and opinions. This exchange requires a time to listen. Listening to what others have to say shows respect and encourages others to listen when you speak.

But, listening is not enough. You must actually hear what is said and not spend your quiet time thinking about what you want to say next. The conversation becomes non-existent at that point. You must pay attention to what is being voiced whether or not you agree with the speaker. Not paying attention is typical of not maturing and typifies a closed mind.

> *A conversation is a dialogue, not a monologue.*
> *That's why there are so few good conversations:*
> *due to scarcity, two intelligent talkers seldom meet.*
> *Truman Capote, 1924–1984*
> *American Writer*

There is a new communication problem we are encountering in this age of technology. Have you ever been in public or attending a social function and people seem to be preoccupied with conversations on their phones? Are they actually talking with a real person about something dreadfully important, or are they checking their social media pages? We are rapidly losing the art of face to face conversation and gaining lower social competencies. Social media is not a good substitute for real relationships with people. It's your choice to live life in the real world or to let technology take over. You won't want to miss out on some good experiences and meaningful relationships.

Employers have been known to look up a current or prospective employee's name on the internet. They discover much about your character in the private sector. Those social networking sites are great for viewing all the info they need to see. Photos you post are out there forever. This can become a nightmare fast. Think before you post.

Take care in what you say or write. Once it's out there, there is no taking it back. Especially with the internet, your words have the ability to spread much further and more permanently than you ever may have intended. Much like a cancer it is difficult to put to an end. Be sure you are willing to deal with the consequences. Don't let it come back and bite you in the behind. It is never worth the price of losing the respect of others and/or your goals.

The real art of conversation is not only to say the right thing in the right place,
but also to leave unsaid the wrong thing at the tempting moment.
Dorothy Nevill, 1826–1913
British Writer

Gossip is a very dangerous beast. It is a source of misinformation and destruction. It can be a slight mention of something innocuous about an individual, place, or event, or something more deliberately vicious. Make judgments concerning such things for yourself. You may miss out on fantastic opportunities to meet people and experience events based on another's motives which are often difficult to discern.

Gossip, n.: Hearing something you like about someone you don't.
Earl Wilson, 1934–2005
American Baseball Pitcher

Frighteningly the damage caused by gossip can be inflicted without the target ever becoming aware that they've been maligned. It's also terrifying how a gossip story can morph and evolve into something not resembling the initial narrative or not even based upon complete and valid facts. Remember the telephone game most of us played as a child? The original sentence never ever came close to the announced ending. Does that make it true or accurate?

What is your response to gossip?

Sometimes it doesn't hurt to verify what you have heard either from a truly discrete person or directly from the victim. But, be sure there is a real need to validate and be tasteful if you chose to do this. In most situations, it is best to leave the matter alone and suggest to the speaker that the statements are inappropriate, inaccurate, or not something in which you want or need to become involve. If people realize that this type of rude behavior is not part of your repertoire, they will avoid it with you. It just may put them on the path to becoming a better person.

The Triple Filter Test
A friend came to Socrates with a juicy bit of gossip.
Socrates replied to him, "Before you tell me this bit of gossip,
will it pass my triple filter test? First, is what you are about to tell me true?"
The man replied that he was not sure;
he had heard it but could not verify its truthfulness.
Socrates continued, "You want to tell me some gossip
but you are not positive that it is true."
"Well," said Socrates, "Is what you are about to tell me good?"
"No," the man replied, "it certainly is not good."
"So," Socrates continued, "you want to tell me something that may not be true
and it certainly is not good. Is what you are about to tell me going to be useful to me?"
Again the man had to confess that no, it would not be useful to Socrates.
So, in his wisdom, Socrates then said,
"Well, if you are not sure it is true, you know it is not good,
and you tell me that it will not be useful to me,
why then tell it to me?"
Attributed to Socrates, 469–399 BC
Classical Greek Philosopher and a Founder of Western Philosophy

It is important to allow others to experience a person or situation without prejudgment or negative influence. You are a better person to keep slanderous opinions, false statements, or inflammatory comments to yourself. Lives can be harmed via any 'poison pen' activity. It is cowardly, nasty, abusive, and purely malicious. Take an honest and careful look at your motives and those of other people.

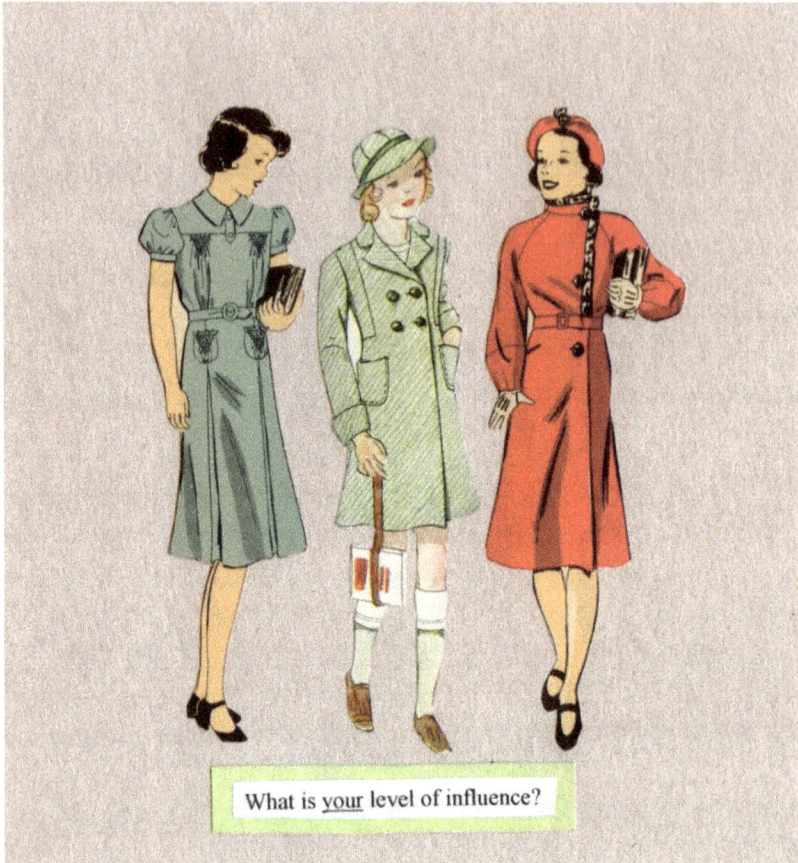

What is <u>your</u> level of influence?

Don't assume malice for what stupidity can explain.
Eponymous Adage or Variation of Heinlein's Razor

If you personally have a problem with someone's behavior or something they said, go directly to them for clarification. You could have misunderstood or misinterpreted the situation or what that person meant. This does not mean that you should be confrontational, but rather inquisitive. It can be a bad idea to chat about the situation with other people first. You could be perceived as delving in gossip, slander, or sabotage. If it matters so much to you, be an adult and show the confidence to approach the individual openly and honestly. Allow for personal growth in both of you.

The most destructive force in the universe is gossip.
Dave Barry, 1947–
American Author and Columnist

You know what they say about glass houses? It takes years to build up trust, and it only takes suspicion, not proof, to destroy it. Defamation of character is a tough thing to overcome. Allow others to discover who they are and to evolve into the best that this can be. You will usually be given the freedom to do the same. Live by example of what you want out of life and from others.

Be consistent in words and actions. Do what you say you will and don't do what you say you won't. Confusion ensues otherwise. Nobody, not even yourself, will know what to expect from you. You become undependable and not well defined in character and values. In the same note, finish what you start or ask for help.

A job worth doing is worth doing well.
Author Unknown

There are three things nobody should ever forget to say: I love you, thank you, and I'm sorry. But, it's not enough to just say them. These words represent thought-ful behavior. So show that you mean what you say. Look people in the eyes when you say them. It may even be appropriate to make physical contact in the form of a hug, hand shake, or pat on the arm.

Mind Your Manners

Manners are of more importance than laws.
Manners are what vex or soothe, corrupt or purify,
exalt or debase, barbarize or refine us,
by a constant, steady, uniform, insensible operation,
like that of the air we breathe in.
Edmund Burke, 1729–1797
Irish Statesman, Author, Political Theorist, and Philosopher

GOOD MANNERS NEVER go out of style. Be patient as it may take practice for some of them to become a natural part of your repertoire. Care enough about how you are perceived by others. The ones that matter are the ones who also behave appropriately as evidenced by the happiness and success in their daily lives. You will find doors opening and opportunities presented with behavior consistent with a mature, caring individual.

More practice definitely...

Respect for ourselves guides our morals;
Respect for others guides are manners.
Laurence Sterne, 1713–1768
Anglo-Irish Novelist and Clergyman

It is wise to model good manners to others. You will tend to get back what others experience you putting out there. In fact, one of the first things we learn as small children is how to say "please" and "thank you." A person can never say this too many times. These simple words tell someone that you appreciate what they do and value their presence in your relationship, no matter how fleeting or permanent. You will discover that it not only shows your respect of others, to others, but will tend to make you feel emotionally and mentally positive as well.

Remember to say "excuse me" and "you're welcome" as appropriate. These simple phrases acknowledge a courtesy towards others for your be- havior. Typically one uses "excuse me" when moving past an individual and perhaps encroaching on personal space. It is also good to use when normal bodily functions interrupt at the wrong moment in public. And "you're wel- come" is a polite way of accepting another person's gratitude for something you've done.

The hardest job kids face today
is learning good manners without seeing any.
Fred Astaire, 1899–1987
American Dancer, Actor, and Choreographer

When approached by someone, look them in the eye and greet them. If a hand shake is appropriate, don't hesitate to offer one. When in conver- sation, be sure to respond clearly to questions with a "yes" or "no" and not merely a nod or silence. "Yeah, yep, nah, and ahuh" can make you seem lazy or uninterested in the person. You are better off not using them. Be polite and show an active interest in an individual that is making the effort and taking their own time to speak with you.

Good manners is the art of making those people easy with whom we converse.
Whoever makes the fewest people uneasy is the best bred in the room.

Jonathan Swift, 1667–1745
Irish Author, Clergyman, and Satirist

Hospitality is an art form for expressing a person's manners. Learn how to be both a good guest and a good host. As a guest, respect the host and the efforts put forth into making your stay a pleasant one. By the same token, the host should learn how to respond to a guest with a polite, welcoming attitude. Both a guest and a host need to appreciate what it takes to share the same space for a period of time, whether for an evening or a week.

Communication is very important for both the guest and the host. Asking permission of the host prior to a guest taking any actions, such as letting the housecat outside or helping oneself to food, are considered crucial and can make or break the visit. The host should be mindful of laying out important information to the guest to eliminate stress for everyone. Every good intention may be tested as a lengthy visit comes to its conclusion. Be prepared for this and arm yourself with good manners.

Hospitality is making your guests feel at home,
even if you wish they were.
Author Unknown

In the 1950's, one could readily ascertain from where a person was raised by their table habits. In today's age of globalization, it's not so evident. None-the-less, table manners can make or break an evening. Classic rules have never gone out of style. Do not attempt to speak with your mouth full or wave utensils around as you make your point. Conversations at mealtime should consist of pleasant topics and nothing that would ruin anyone's appetite. Eat slowly and cut food into small bites. It's better for the digestion and eliminates the choking thing …

Manners are a sensitive awareness of the feelings of others.
If you have that awareness, you have good manners, no matter what fork you use.
Emily Post, 1872–1960
American Author of Social Etiquette

The Mind

WHEN DO WE become adults? Adulthood is a never ending development of maturity in how we think, what we say, and the actions we take as a result. It is a growth and expansion in thought, word, and behavior. You have a thoughtful choice in the use of words and actions. Are you stagnant or evolving? Can you make the intuitive connections that will bring about your desired life?

> *People often say that this or that person has not yet found himself.*
> *But the self is not something one finds,*
> *it is something one creates.*
> *Thomas Stephen Szasz, 1920–2012*
> *Hungarian Psychiatrist, Academic, and Author*

Rational thought is an advanced thinking skill that is developed with experience and practice. Children are concrete thinkers. Abstract thinking emerges as an individual grows towards adulthood. Drugs and alcohol are known to cause developmental delays in both emotional and intellectual maturity. Development ceases at the point where drug abuse begins and does not resume until it stops. Cognitive insight and intuition are privileged to adults and damaged by such abuses to the mind.

> *Intellectual growth should commence at birth*
> *and cease only at death.*
> *Albert Einstein, 1879–1955*
> *German born American Noble Prize-Winning Physicist*

With age, <u>does not</u> naturally come wisdom. To be thirty or forty or seventy does not mean that an individual has 'absorbed' the necessary information to think or behave in an adult-like manner or make decisions that are necessary to function successfully and productively. To put it simply, adults set good examples that others admire.

A boy becomes an adult three years before his parents think he does,
and about two years after he thinks he does.
Lewis B. Hershey, 1893–1977
United States Four-Star General

At the same time, keep in mind that behaving as an adult does not mean that one should forget how to be a child. Maintain a youthful perspective. Incorporating that youth into 'right' thinking leads to good character and usually success in family life and career. We can take much from our lessons as children and teenagers. Retaining youth is important. It's what keeps a person vital and exciting, providing the right environment for creativity and insight.

If a child is to keep alive his inborn sense of wonder
without any such gift from the fairies,
he needs the companionship of at least one adult who can share it,
rediscovering with him the joy, excitement
and mystery of the world we live in.
Rachel Carson, 1907–1964
American Writer, Biologist, and Ecologist

Life is not a 'race' but a meandering journey that takes each of us to different places. It's more than acceptable to have fun in the process of exploring the world and who you are in it.

If it weren't for the rocks in the bed,
the stream would have no song.
Carl Perkins, 1932–1998
American Musician

Values are instilled in the early years of life. They grow and evolve, mostly after the teen years. Look for the red flags. Anything that makes one's internal instinct shout "what the heck …?" is something to pause and evaluate prior to any involvement. Listen to your gut feelings. It could save you in so many ways.

What fails to kill me, only makes me stronger.
Friedrich Nietzsche, 1844–1900
German Philosopher and Classical Philologist

I am passionate about my music …

Dissatisfaction equals the need for change. If something doesn't work, do something different. If pessimism is the seed of failure, which is paralyzing, then passion is the boost to action. Be passionate about something. Find a hobby or activity that is satisfying and positive. What you puts into your life is frequently that thing from which you can benefit. Be enthusiastic about life and what you are doing or change what you are doing.

A cloud does not know why it moves in such a direction and at such a speed.
It feels an impulsion,
this is the way to go now.
But the sky knows the reasons and the patterns behind the clouds
and you will know too,
when you lift yourself high enough to see beyond horizons.
Richard Bach, 1936–
American Writer

If you find yourself lacking in something or 'stuck,' find out what it is that you need in order to move forward. If you have trouble in a school subject or task at work, get help. It's out there in many ways and from many sources. Don't stagnate. Don't be afraid to try new things.

Break the Pattern

Never hesitate to seek out counseling for any issues weighing on your mind. It will offer you a perfect opportunity to step back and evaluate any life situation before taking any action. A counselor acts as a neutral party that serves as a sounding board for your thoughts and emotions without passing judgment. It's often a better choice than using a well-meaning friend.

Great minds have purposes, others have wishes.
Washington Irving, 1783–1859
American Author and Historian

Attitude is contagious. Try consciously observing its effects sometime. Ever gone into a social situation, whether it is a one on one with a complete stranger or group of friends and noticed how a smile or pleasant word can set the mood? Ever heard a smile on the telephone? Control your attitude or it will control you.

The 92-year-old, petite, well-poised and proud lady, who is fully dressed each morning by eight o'clock, with her hair fashionably coifed and makeup perfectly applied, even though she is legally blind, moved to a nursing home today.
Her husband of 70 years recently passed away, making the move necessary.
After many hours of waiting patiently in the lobby of the nursing home, she smiled sweetly when told her room was ready.
As she maneuvered her walker to the elevator, I provided a visual description of her tiny room, including the eyelet sheets that had been hung on her window.
"I love it," she stated with the enthusiasm of an eight-year-old having just been presented with a new puppy.
"Mrs. Jones, you haven't seen the room … just wait."
"That doesn't have anything to do with it," she replied. "Happiness is something you decide on ahead of time. Whether I like my room or not doesn't depend on how the furniture is arranged … it's how I arrange my mind.
I already decided to love it. It's a decision I make every morning when I wake up. I have a choice; I can spend the day in bed recounting the difficulty I have with the parts of my body that no longer work, or get out of bed and be thankful for the ones that do.
Each day is a gift, and as long as my eyes open I'll focus on the new day and all the happy memories I've stored away just for this time in my life."
Old age is like a bank account … you withdraw from what you've put in.

So, my advice to you would be to deposit a lot of happiness
in the bank account of memories.
Author Unknown

Self-actualization is discovering who you are and what you can be. What are the limits to your ability to live your life the way you want? This journey through life is an adventure towards developing the self and being happy with it. Can you sit alone in a room? Or do you have to have other people around. It's important to be comfortable with who you are and easier to see who you want to become when the environment is relatively quiet.

With your own hands, carve out your destiny.
Guru Nanak, 1469–1539
Indian Teacher and Founder of Sikhism

I'm taking a journey of discovery
along the spiritual path of enlightenment.

Maturity is not a sign of age, but rather a level of enlightenment achieved in varying degrees. Enlightenment is the goal of the spiritual path. It gives your life meaning within the whole. Find the connection with yourself and others. Your life can be changed by people who don't even know you. Study the various philosophies of those sages who have come before and have found answers to those burning questions we all ask. Learning, educating ourselves is the only way, the only course to finding what it means to become a happy and successful adult, living life to the fullest. This enlightenment of the self or the illumination of reality is a marvelous 'ah-ha' moment.

A man who knows others is wise.
A man who knows himself is enlightened.
Lao Tzu, 604–531 BC
Chinese Philosopher and Father of Taoism

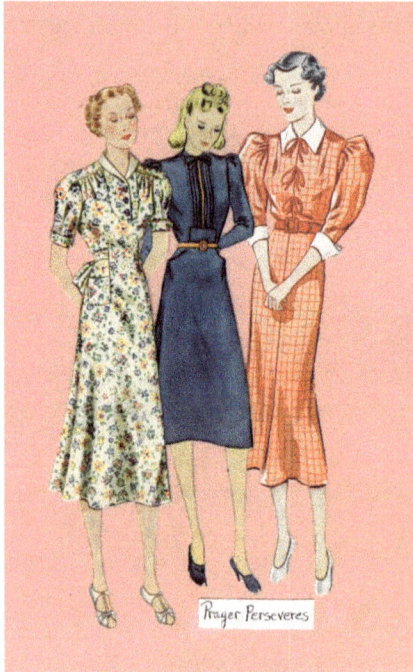

Prayer Perseveres

What is your spiritual path? This refers to the evolution of consciousness or the intellectual refinement of thought and feeling as it pertains not to the body or things of substance, but rather the intellect of the soul. The path can be found through endless sources: religion, yoga, long walks, meditation, et cetera. Find the one (or more) that works for you. You will find it provides a sense of calmness, a peace of mind. A sanctuary for your consciousness.

Meditation is a quiet reflection or contemplation of what we experience in life. Many psychologists will argue that everybody participates in meditation during REM sleep. The fast learners include time for this during the waking hours as well.

The Five Meditations
From The Gospel of Buddha

There are five meditations. The first meditation is the meditation of love in which thou must so adjust thy heart that thou longest for the weal and welfare of all beings, including the happiness of thine enemies.

The second meditation is the meditation of pity, in which thou thinkest of all beings in distress, vividly representing in thine imagination their sorrows and anxieties so as to arouse a deep compassion for them in thy soul.

The third meditation is the meditation of joy, in which thou thinkest of the prosperity of others and rejoicest with their rejoicings.

The fourth meditation is the meditation on purity, in which thou considerest the evil consequences of corruption, the effects of wrongs and evils.

How trivial is often the pleasure of the moment and how fatal are its consequences.

The fifth meditation is the meditation on serenity, in which thou risest above love and hate, tyranny and thralldom, wealth and want, and regardest thine own fate with impartial calmness and perfect tranquility.

Compiled from ancient records by Paul Carus, 1852–1919
German-American Author, Theologian, and Professor of Philosophy

The Body

CONFUCIUS BELIEVED THAT he body and the mind are equally important. Diet directly affects the mind/body connection. Mental acuity and awareness, physical activity level and drive, emotions, and chemical levels in the body are all interrelated and altered by what we consume and inhale. Additionally, keeping active helps to maintain the balance achieved with proper nutrition.

It is not difficult to eat the right foods. You will find it to be healthier and much less expensive to eat at home. Some individuals will enjoy the novelty in using or creating recipes for meals. There are so many that can be created ahead of time to use later in the week. If you have roommates, consider splitting up the meal preparation or work together. It can be a healthy bonding time and an opportunity to catch up with busy lives.

All over the world, good relations begin with the breaking of bread …

Crisp Apple Salad
3 crisp apples cored and sliced
¼ cup crumbled blue cheese
5 T coarsely chopped walnuts
1/3 cup light olive oil
1 ½ T lemon juice
4 cups lightly packed lettuce mix

A good rule of thumb is to create a grocery list prior to shopping. Make a list of the meals for the week and create a shopping list from this. It will enable you to see that all of the food groups, especially nutritional whole foods, are in your diet. You will also be able to identify which ingredients that may already be in the cupboard or refrigerator. This saves money.

I was 32 when I started cooking;
up until then, I just ate.
Julia Child, 1912–2004
American Chef, Author, Television Personality

Whole, unprocessed foods will keep you healthy. Look up some of the ingredients on containers of the products you buy. This may scare you. An excellent guide to follow is that if you can't pronounce it, why would you eat it?

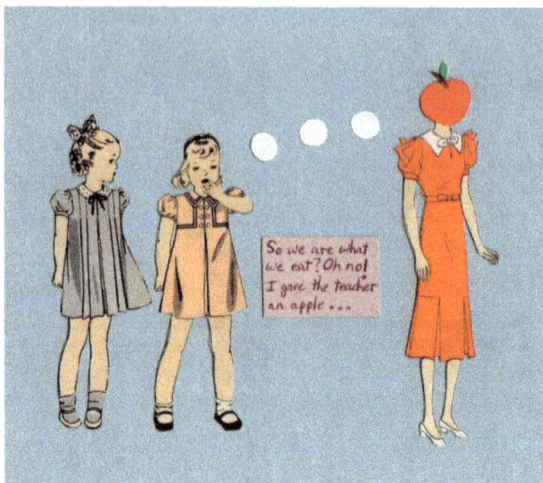

There is a serious issue that concerns those individuals who have eating disorders. While there are several different ones, two of most commonly heard about are bulimia and anorexia. These two problems are typically tied to an individual's concept of body image.

Blame is not difficult to assign. Yet it's so very odd how society has evolved in its definition of a healthy and attractive "look" throughout the centuries. Just be certain that help is out there for you … Or be that caring friend or family member and get help for someone else who needs it.

'The Freshman Fifteen' is a popular term that is often heard about an individual's weight gain after the first year at college. Living away from some of the family regulations on food intake, many of us finally get the opportunity to delve into the enormous world of junk food. Others merely rely on a snacking or fast food diet because of the time constraints of work or school. There is also typically less incentive to make the time to work out. Adjust your food intake and find time to exercise. Just do it. Walks after school or work can have great advantages.

Insanity: doing the same thing over and over again
and expecting different results.
Albert Einstein, 1879–1955
German Theoretical Physicist

Get out of the house! Check out your local Y or other community and college facilities. Join activity clubs such as fencing, aerobics, yoga, swimming, kayaking, volleyball, slow-pitch ball ... the list is endless. These offer a great way to keep fit and to meet people outside of your typical work and school environments. Your overall physical and mental health will be better. The more active you are, the more energy you will find that you have. It can help to regenerate your mind and to think in more creative ways at work or school.

So much to do and so very little time ...

If it weren't for the fact that the TV set and the refrigerator are so far apart,
some of us wouldn't get any exercise at all.
Joey Adams, 1911–1999
American Comedian and Author

Alcohol and/or drug intake often accompany the new found freedom away from the watchful eyes of parents. Such activities will guarantee a dramatic increase or decrease in your weight and reduce your physical and mental well-being. Even in moderation some individuals can face drastic changes in their metabolism and overall health. This can mean permanent damage to one's health, as well as personal and professional relationships. Instead, get your "rush" from physical activities with your friends …

Too many people confine their exercise to jumping to conclusions,
running off at the mouth, stretching the truth, bending over backwards,
lying down on the job, side stepping responsibility,
swimming against the current and pushing their luck.
Unknown Author

What happened to the knowledge most of us were given about proper eating and the five food groups? Contrary to many a belief, vodka and beer are not adequate members of a food group. Adding a lime to either is not a great way to add fruit to your diet. Individuals tend to eat more junk food with liquor and marijuana use. The munchies will usually make you fat. At the opposite end, very little tends to be eaten under the influence of amphetamine type drugs. We all know that the emaciated look is not stylish.

Smoking cigarettes is rapidly becoming banned in most public places. Several pages could be devoted to merely listing the damage it causes to a person's body. It is not glamorous and slows down the process of realizing most of your goals. It is financially draining, physically damaging, and time consuming.

Get active.
Get outdoors.

Reversal of the physical and social effects due to drug and alcohol abuse can be difficult and sometimes impossible. Right now, take a look at the people that surround you on a daily basis. Do they care about the damage you may be causing yourself? Are they fostering your party mode? Do you have friends who promote sober activities? Avoid facilitators who encourage or permit behaviors that are detrimental or potentially harmful to you and your future. Care enough about yourself to find other, more healthy and interesting activities and friends.

You're not drunk if you can lie on the floor without holding on.
Dean Martin, 1917–1995
American Singer, Actor, and Comedian

Don't Fall Down the Rabbit Hole …

Never get into a vehicle while you or anyone else is under the influence of any drug or alcohol. Never. Never. Never. The price is extremely high. Nobody wants to deal with the enormous list of potential consequences. Sadly, these always radiate throughout the lives of so many innocent people. Use your common sense and knowledge to ditch any car keys and make the time to sleep it off, whether it's you or someone else that needs to do so. This decision will follow you the rest of your life …

Giving Back

GIVING CAN TAKE on many forms, but it should never be about keeping score with money or public recognition. It really concerns an individual's self-worth and value to society. Both of these can be defined by the behavior and the attitude an individual brings to specific situations that truly meet the needs of others.

My country is the world,
And my religion is to do good.
Thomas Paine, 1737–1809
English Writer

Donations of time or finances are the most common forms of our giving back to others. We often feel better after doing so. But, are these actions truly the giving of yourself to others? More often, these methods tend to focus on the betterment of society as a whole instead of more personal, individual needs. Identify who needs you and what you can do to help.

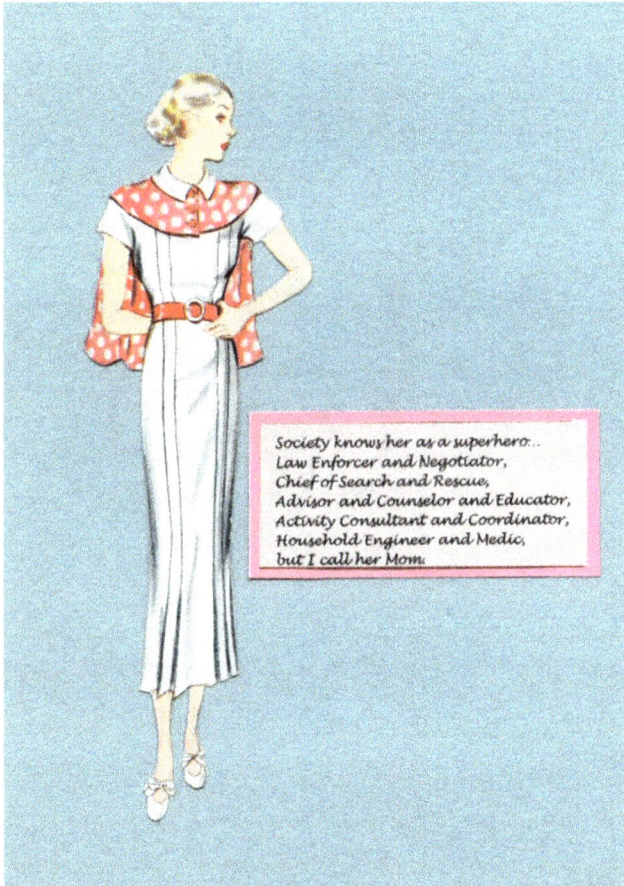

One does not need to risk life and limb to be a hero. A true hero acts in the best interest of another person without expectations of public applause or monetary gain. Some are individuals who may never be noticed for their intentional voluntary deeds. Yet, there are other heroes who find themselves suddenly and unintentionally thrust into a moment when they must think and act with spontaneity. Society must have both types of heroes.

Each have the characteristic of putting others needs before their own, which lends hope for the future of humanity.

The unintentional heroes are the ones that tend to be noticed more by us, because the media jumps on reporting such actions. It seems as though we are witnessing an increase in such spontaneous acts of heroism. Hopefully it is not simply the media's change in focus, which is not necessarily a bad thing. People often need reminders of the good results in performing selfless acts.

Heroes are people who do what has to be done
when it needs to be done, regardless of the consequences.
Author Unknown

It is sad that what is becoming a rare form of giving today is the reaching out beyond ourselves through the simple act of being courteous. Courtesy is giving. Respect of self and others is reflected in our courtesy. It's not just important to help those who may need genuine assistance. The opportunity to act with kindness and respect can be found everywhere:

- allowing a person to go in front of you in the grocery store checkout when they have so few items and you have a full cart
- permitting a car to merge safely in front of you when you see their signal of intent
- being on time to meetings, lunches, or parties
- holding a door open
- giving up your seat to someone on the bus.

The list is endless ... It's what you choose to do in any given situation that makes the difference. This difference can have far reaching positive results not only for an individual and society, but for you. Who have you influenced or made a positive impact upon today?

What we do for ourselves dies with us.
What we do for others and the world remains and is immortal.
Albert Pine, 1861–1937
American Author

In The End …

THERE IS LITTLE doubt that you have found some useful information here. We can all learn so much from other people, both present and past. Don't ever be afraid or hesitant to search for the answers you need. They are out there. Ultimately it's your responsibility to make your life everything you want it to be. And, with the establishment of a good base of knowledge, you will be able to create a starting point from which to move forward through life with greater ease.

Life can only be understood backwards;
but it must be lived forwards.
Søren Kierkegaard, 1813–1855
Danish Philosopher, Theologian, and the Father of Existentialism

Some days you feel like the cat,
and some days you feel like the dog …

Life is a journey of self. It is the development of one's full potential as a human being; the dynamic defining of one's self. The path is replete with possibilities if you can distinguish between what is real and not real. You must question assumptions and dissolve barriers. You will need to release your old roles and self-defeating thoughts and behaviors. Your evolution towards a healthy self-esteem will create a positive self-concept presented to all and will result in you reaching your desired goals. Remember to always be true to yourself. Self-approval equals self-confidence. It's important to be satisfied with who you are while on the journey to becoming what you want to be. Either appreciate who you are or change the things you don't like.

Before you speak, listen.
Before you write, think.
Before you spend, earn.
Before you invest, investigate.
Before you criticize, wait.
Before you pray, forgive.
Before you quit, try.
Before you retire, save.
Before you die, give.
William A. Ward, 1921–1994
American Inspirational Author

Make good use of 'I statements' in your decisions. Own what you think, say, and do. All thoughts, words, and actions have results that will affect your world. Therefore they require thoughtful reflection and a quiet introspection of motives and the numerous possible consequences. This will help you avoid the repercussions that can halt your forward momentum. You are responsible for yourself. You must be able to trust yourself.

How do you know you've become an adult? Think about everything before you say it. Think about everything before you do it. Is it beneficial? Does it hurt someone? If you can answer these questions honestly, then you will know you are an adult. When you can think quickly about the repercussions or results and make a good judgment call … that's when you can think like an adult, respond like an adult, and be considered an adult by those important people in life. Anyone who thinks otherwise is not an adult. It takes practice and will come easily to you with time.

A child becomes an adult when he realizes
that he has a right not only to be right
but also to be wrong.
Thomas Stephen Szasz, 1920–2012
Hungarian Psychiatrist, Academic, and Author

There are things that will throw you off. But know that you can conquer every obstacle that comes your way. You can always improve your situation. It takes knowledge, good judgment, and perseverance to get through everyday living. Adults know this. We all have our battle scars. The reality is what we do with the lessons learned.

It's not the years in your life that count.
It's the life in your years.
Abraham Lincoln, 1809–1865
16th United States President

Happiness is a journey, not a destination …

Through the positive development of your attitude, common sense, and observational skills you will have opportunities to achieve not only your desired goals, but perhaps things beyond any of your wildest dreams. Manifest your destiny. The world doesn't stop for you. It is your choice to get on and to have a great ride. Believe in your ability to have an exciting adventure while allowing others to have the same chance for a great future. A guarantee of happiness is then possible. Now that you have a clue as to how to begin or continue your fantastic journey, remember to **always protect your behind …**

He has achieved success who has lived well, laughed often and loved much;
who has gained the respect of intelligent men and the love of little children;
who has filled his niche and accomplished his task;
who has left the world better than he found it,
whether by an improved poppy, a perfect poem, or a rescued soul;
who has never lacked appreciation of earth's beauty or failed to express it;
who has always looked for the best in others and given them the best he had;
whose life was an inspiration;
whose memory a benediction.
Bessie Stanley
Brown Book Magazine Competition 1904

Fascinated by human behavior since early childhood, Barbara began collecting historical quotes on the effects of mankind's thoughts, words, and actions. She was amazed as to how people throughout time continue to make the same mistakes over and over again. It was the reading through of this collection that ultimately led her to the creation of the book "Always Protect Your Behind: A Life Guide for Young Adults or Misguided Old Ones."

Barbara holds undergraduate degrees in Psychology and Anthropology, a Masters in Counseling and a degree in Paralegal Studies. She is a Nationally Certified Mental Health Counselor and currently resides in Southern California.

www.ingramcontent.com/pod-product-compliance
Lightning Source LLC
LaVergne TN
LVHW022011080426
835513LV00009B/671